Open Arms, Safe Communities

OPEN ARMS, SAFE COMMUNITIES

The Theology of Church Security

JEANIE GARRETT

CHURCH
PUBLISHING
INCORPORATED

Unless otherwise noted, the Scripture quotations are from New Revised Standard Version Bible, copyright © 1989 National Council of the Churches of Christ in the United States of America. Used by permission. All rights reserved worldwide.

Scripture marked NASB are quotations taken from the (NASB®) New American Standard Bible®, Copyright © 1960, 1971, 1977, 1995, 2020 by The Lockman Foundation. Used by permission. All rights reserved. www.lockman.org.

Scripture quotations marked (NIV) are taken from the Holy Bible, New International Version®, NIV®. Copyright © 1973, 1978, 1984, 2011 by Biblica, Inc.™ Used by permission of Zondervan. All rights reserved worldwide. www.zondervan.com. The "NIV" and "New International Version" are trademarks registered in the United States Patent and Trademark Office by Biblica, Inc.™

Church Publishing
19 East 34th Street
New York, NY 10016
www.churchpublishing.org

Cover design by Paul Soupiset, Soupiset Design
Typeset by Denise Hoff

Library of Congress Cataloging-in-Publication Data

Names: Garrett, Jeanie, author.
Title: Open arms, safe communities : the theology of church security / Jeanie Garrett.
Description: New York, NY : Church Publishing, [2021]
Identifiers: LCCN 2021009514 (print) | LCCN 2021009515 (ebook) | ISBN 9781640653221 (paperback) | ISBN 9781640653214 (epub)
Subjects: LCSH: Church management. | Church buildings--Security measures. | Church buildings--Safety measures.
Classification: LCC BV652.9 .G37 2021 (print) | LCC BV652.9 (ebook) | DDC 254--dc23
LC record available at https://lccn.loc.gov/2021009514
LC ebook record available at https://lccn.loc.gov/2021009515

CONTENTS

When I set out to write this book, I found myself asking, "How did we get to this point?" By "this point" I mean, how did we get to the place where thousands of people walk into places of worship each week and wonder if their congregation will be the next one to appear on the evening news? Religious spaces are by their nature soft targets. We go to church to worship and pray; fears and concerns are usually checked at the door, and weapons are often prohibited. By design, we feel emotionally and physically safe. Unfortunately, these reasons make our sacred spaces ideal for someone wanting to do tremendous damage in a short amount of time. When we learn of the latest shooting at a house of worship, so many questions race through our mind. What religion or denomination was targeted? What kind of gun was it, and how did that person obtain it? Mostly, though, I think we ask ourselves, why did this happen?

In my search for answers, I didn't expect the facts to so quickly and undeniably point to the rise of white supremacy in our country. While it's not the *only* factor, I do believe it is by far the biggest one and must be part of the discussion of mass shootings in our places of worship.

Speaking on the 2019 panel "Targeting the Sacred: When Houses of Worship Come Under Attack," Yolanda Pierce, dean of the Howard University School of Divinity, said:

> This is about power. It's about who is on the under-
> side of history. You attack where people are most
> vulnerable because you're sending the message that

no matter how long you've been in this country, no
matter what gains you have made in this country,
we will always make you feel vulnerable, and we
will always enforce a kind of second-class citizen-
ship because you're always in danger, and so you
attack at the churches because they are the sacred
spaces of most people's identity.[1]

Brette Steele, who is the director of prevention and national
security at the McCain Institute for International Leadership in
Arizona and former deputy director of the US Countering Violent
Extremism Task Force, also appeared on this panel. Steele says that
unlike the days of clandestine meetings of Ku Klux Klan members
who planned their attacks on Black churches in person, the explo-
sion of the internet has allowed lone actors to find online communities that either support the ideology they already have or introduce
them to a new one. This was certainly the case for Dylann Roof,
the twenty-one-year-old who killed nine people during a Bible
study at the historic Mother Emanuel African Methodist Episcopal
Church in Charleston, South Carolina, in 2015. According to Arno
Michaelis, a former skinhead who speaks openly about his con-
version away from white supremacy, these kind of websites inten-
tionally make outcasts like Roof feel valued and important while
indoctrinating them with anti-Christian messages and beliefs.[2]
Roof, who posted under the screen name Lil Aryan on the neo-
Nazi site Stormfront,[3] self-radicalized from the privacy and comfort of his home. According to Steele,

Historically there were password protected Al
Qaida sites, and you had to know someone to get
into them. It's simply not true anymore. . . . It is
much easier for people to find violent extremist
content now than it was twenty years ago. No question. Lone actors may be very much a part of a community in participating in a broader conversation
online. It's just that their attack planning is more

to themselves. In terms of group coordinated and
directed action, you almost never see that anymore.[4]

On its website, the Anti-Defamation League lists more than two
hundred groups, symbols, and logos that represent white supremacy
in the United States. Following the 2017 Unite the Right rally at
the University of Virginia in Charlottesville, when hundreds of
white supremacists marched in the streets and twenty-year-old
James Alex Fields Jr. rammed his car into a crowd of counterpro-
testers, killing Heather Heyer and injuring nineteen others, the
increase in incidents and threats of white supremacy became something the Department of Homeland Security could no longer turn
a blind eye to. In the fall of 2019, then acting secretary of homeland
security Kevin McAleenan described white nationalism as one of
the most dangerous threats to the United States, despite a report
ten years earlier from his own department warning that the election of an African American president could fuel white supremacy
extremism.[5]

McAleenan's assertion came as the Committee on Oversight and
Reform concluded a three-part hearing before the Subcommittee
on Civil Rights and Civil Liberties that same year. The hearings
were aimed at and titled "Confronting Violent White Supremacy,"
and they brought many troubling concerns to light. Most of the
committee members and witnesses who testified agreed that white
supremacy had risen to an alarming level. Chairman Jamie Raskin
(D-MD), who would later lead the House impeachment trial
against former president Donald Trump following the January 6,
2021, attack on the Capitol, called it "the most significant threat
of domestic terror in the United States" today.[6] He was not alone
in this assertion. Chairman Stephen Lynch (D-MA) noted in his
opening statement at the third hearing, "In recent years we've seen
white supremacists increasingly resorting to the use of violence to
achieve their ideological objectives. And today, for the first time
since September 11, 2001, more people have been killed in racially
motivated or right-wing terrorist incidents in the United States
than in attacks perpetrated by Islamic extremists."[7] As early as

2010, local law enforcement agencies were pushing aside govern-ment-driven reports on ISIS and Al Qaeda and asking the FBI and Homeland Security how to deal with the skinhead groups surfacing in their communities.[8] With cases on the rise, problems with the classification and reporting of incidents became obvious. The term "domestic terrorism" was often used when describing such attacks; however, the FBI did not call the mass shootings at the Mother Emanuel AME Church, the Tree of Life synagogue in Pittsburgh, or the murder of Heather Heyer domestic terrorism. Why not? Could it be because those perpetrators were white?[9]

Omar Ricci was one of many witnesses who testified before the Committee on Oversight and Reform during these hearings. Ricci is the chairman of the Islamic Center of Southern California and past chairman of the Muslim Public Affairs Council. He is also a reserve officer with the Los Angeles Police Department. In written testimony submitted May 15, 2019, Ricci discussed his own experi-ence with white supremacy threats, including feces-smeared pages of the Quran mailed to him after President Trump was inaugurated. Ricci explained how mosques, synagogues, and churches, feeling particularly vulnerable to an attack, are being forced to reallocate the little money they have to security measures: "It has forced a cul-ture of a mosque being an open space for those seeking community and spirituality to adapt a tactical mindsight and have active shooter trainings."[10] The monetary cost of protecting its members to ensure a safe place to gather, pray, and worship most certainly pales in com-parison to the emotional price of constantly worrying that loved ones are not safe.

In the summer of 2020, the Black Lives Matter movement forced many of us to take a deeper look at systemic racism within our cul-ture as well as within some police departments, including the very departments we call on to protect our churches. Just days into 2021, the world watched as thousands of insurgents, some of them car-rying Confederate flags, pushed their way past police and took over the US Capitol, one of our nation's *most* sacred spaces. These events continued to answer my question, "How did we get here?" which I felt was essential to knowing before fully understanding how we can move toward a safer future.

In the coming chapters, we will focus on topics and conversations that are imperative to formulating a plan that is right for your faith community. We will unpack our fears—both bad and good kinds— and examine how places of worship are making decisions around guns. We will take an intimate look at the effects that mass tragedy has on congregations and how to move forward in the wake of these shootings as we seek to balance the tensions between our call to protect and our call to welcome. I will then walk you through a step-by-step process of creating a sensible security plan (and the pitfalls to avoid!) that reflects our shared commitment to God, our faith, and our congregations. Lastly, we will take a hard look at the communities outside our church walls and assess how we can stand up and speak out to create a safer place for all of God's children.

CHAPTER 1

What Are We Afraid Of?

When I sit down to work with a church security task force, I like to ask, "What are you afraid of?" The answers vary but almost always involve a mass shooting.

"I'm afraid I won't know what to do."

"I'm afraid someone I love will be shot."

"I'm afraid I will die."

Presbyterian pastor Joseph Moore says these sentiments echo many of the conversations he's had over the years, the most memorable being the time an older parishioner invited him out to eat. As they eased into the meal, she confessed, "And now I need to tell you why I *really* wanted you to come to lunch. I'm scared. I'm scared to come to church." Knowing almost nothing he said would change the emotional response she had to the most recent church shooting, he asked her to tell him everything she was afraid of. "And I just sat and listened to her talk about her fears that someone was going to come into the church and shoot it up," Moore said. "It was one of those conversations where I realized statistics don't speak to fear."[1]

Fear is one of the most powerful forces in our lives. It pushes past logic and engages the part of us that is not our best selves. As theologian and ethicist Scott Bader-Saye notes in his book *Formed by Love*, when fear overwhelms us, it can lead us to justify preemptive violence, deny hospitality to the stranger, and forgo generosity.

"Our moral lives become fundamentally disordered when fear takes control. . . . This is not what God created us to be."[2] But it is important to note that fear and uncertainty are among the most universal problems human beings face, and the Bible constantly depicts that. Author and pastor Ellen Debenport writes that every time angels show up on the scene, they are telling the humans they encounter, "Fear not," because "[a]ngels must understand the reflexive fear in human beings pretty well."[3] This same fear is reflected all the way through the Bible, from the first created humans, who hide from the God they have disobeyed in Genesis 3:10, to Moses, who rejects God's call to return to Egypt in Exodus 4, to the psalmist constantly fearing for his life ("Be gracious to me, O LORD, for I am languishing; / O LORD, heal me, for my bones are shaking with terror," Psalm 6:2). The New Testament offers the archangel Gabriel asking Mary to carry the Son of God (and again, to fear not); Peter, the headstrong disciple of Jesus so fearful that three times he denies the person he loves most; and, depending on the gospel and your theology, Jesus himself in the Garden of Gethsemane even wrestles with continuing forward on a path that will lead to his torture and death. Fear has been a powerful and present force in human life since the beginning of time. It is all very well for the writer of 1 John to suggest that perfect love casts out fear, but it is much harder to achieve that perfect love, or to find the proper balance of faith and fear. Scripture and Christian theology return to this problem again and again because it is so deeply human to get caught up in fear, even if that fear is unwarranted.

This fear and anxiety explains why many well-intentioned church security task force teams start strong then dissolve before the work is complete. People don't want to think or talk about worst-case scenarios, especially on a routine basis at a weekly meeting. Starting with the simple but powerful question, "What are you afraid of?" allows us to put into words the feelings that seem too overwhelming or too scary to deal with in our mind. (As everyone in my house can tell you, "naming your Voldemort" is an important step in chipping away at the power of fear!) By taking a more realistic look at what we are afraid of and the weight we give it, we are able to move past the unspeakable and begin having important, constructive conversations about the work ahead.

Excessive and Unhealthy Fear

I decided to dig deep into this idea of how our fears shape the security work houses of worship choose to do or, in some cases, not do. I was frequently flying for work during this time and looked forward to the endless hours I could spend reading research on the plane. On one particular trip, my book of choice was Bader-Saye's *Following Jesus in a Culture of Fear*. It wasn't lost on me that the book's original cover (the one I was holding) was of an airport security checkpoint. On several occasions I considered whether the person sitting next to me wondered why in the world I would choose *that* to read on a plane of all places. At the same time, I was acutely aware that with all the dangers we knowingly face and all the worst-case scenarios we could imagine, there we all were flying from city to city, trusting that dozens of things that could go wrong wouldn't. As Bader-Saye writes:

> We need some clear, sensible reflection on fear— how to acknowledge it without being manipulated by it, how to resist it without assuming we should (or could) be fearless, how to receive it as a gift without letting it dominate our lives. This is especially important among Christians who seek to follow Jesus, for Jesus does not promise safety.[4]

Every day we take risks—like driving a car or climbing a ladder— that we know could result in an accident. However, most of us have done these things hundreds if not thousands of times with no harm, so our expected sense of safety is high. Let's apply this "expected sense of safety" to going to church and our fear of a mass shooting while there. The FBI tracks active shooting incidents and releases statistics once compiled. Of the 305 active shootings that took place from 2000 to 2019 (the most recent year available), thirteen were at places of worship—that's about 4 percent of the incidents, falling significantly behind schools of all academic levels (20 percent), and shootings at businesses (44 percent).[5] Statistically, the chances are low that our place of worship will come under attack. In fact, shootings at worship sites makes up the lowest percent of all the categories. However—and this is a big however—in the cases where shootings have happened in faith-based locations, the casualties are often high and the violation of people's sense of community, safety, and religion felt so deeply that the emotional impact is huge.

Take the shooting at Mother Emanuel Church. Nine people were killed at this revered and historic African American church after gunman Dylann Roof quietly sat through Bible study with those he was about to murder. During the shooting, he screamed racial slurs and tormented his victims as many of them lay dying. He later wrote from jail, "I would like to make it crystal clear, I do not regret what I did."[6] I'm not sure what of all that is the most terrifying part. I believe the depth of the fear that spreads over us is most likely in response to the horrific nature of the shooting in such a sacred place rather than the precise number of lives lost.

Natalie Barden, sister of Daniel Barden, who died in his first-grade classroom at Sandy Hook Elementary, understands and describes the all-consuming fear and utter violation of one's sense of safe places: "Most people go through life thinking, 'It could never happen to me.' But I know that it could, because it happened to Daniel. I could be in the most relaxing place and still worry that someone with a gun could come up and shoot me."[7] Freelance writer Steve Neumann described his constant fear in a 2015 article for Vox.com:

> I now feel uneasy in all public spaces. When my girlfriend and I went to see *Mission: Impossible—Rogue Nation* on opening day we were running a little late, so we had to sit in the front row. It had only been a week since a gunman shot two women in a Louisiana movie theater. I felt exposed and cast a quick glance at any person who walked in late,

anyone who got up to pee. I told myself that if it looked like anyone was reaching for a gun, I'd bum rush him before he had a chance to get a shot off. I stopped holding my girlfriend's hand because my palms were so sweaty.[8]

While we can certainly understand and may even experience the fear and anxiety Barden and Neumann describe, it's imperative that we work to harness it and not allow it to lead or control. In the twentieth chapter of the Gospel of John, we find Jesus's disciples locked behind doors after he has been crucified, paralyzed with fear. They cannot continue to do the work that Jesus left for them, even though among his final words to them were, "Do not let your hearts be troubled, and do not let them be afraid."[9]

Theologians have long written about fear and its effects on us. Thomas Aquinas taught that fear is born of love and, as Bader-Saye writes, is the imagination of a future evil:

> So, how do we know when fear is excessive? According to Aquinas, "Reason dictates that certain goods are to be sought after more than certain evils are to be avoided. Accordingly when the appetite shuns what the reason dictates that we should endure rather than forfeit others that we should rather seek for, fear is inordinate and sinful." Aquinas gets a bit complicated here, but he's simply saying that we fear excessively when we allow the avoidance of evil to eclipse the pursuit of good. When we fear excessively we live in a mode of reacting to and plotting against evil rather than actively doing what is right. Excessive fear causes our scope of vision to narrow, when it needs to be enlarged.[10]

This isn't to say there isn't healthy fear and real warning signs we should adhere to, but an unhealthy fear consumes us unnecessarily and, ultimately, can destroy us. German theologian Dietrich

Bonhoeffer spoke of the dangers of *giving into* fear in a 1933 sermon. Hitler was moving into power, the Hindenburg government was on the verge of falling, and Nazism was spreading. No one, including Bonhoeffer, knew what was to come.

> Fear is, somehow or other, the archenemy itself. It crouches in people's hearts. It hollows out their insides, until their resistance and strength are spent and they suddenly break down. Fear secretly gnaws and eats away at all the ties that bind a person to God and to others, and when in a time of need that person reaches for those ties and clings to them, they break and the individual sinks back into himself or herself, helpless and despairing, while hell rejoices.[11]

"In other words," as president of the Bonhoeffer Institute Rob Scheck writes, "because we are afraid, we will think, say, or do something that we wouldn't otherwise. The sobering reality is that whatever we fear will effectively dominate us."[12] Here is where Moses would have been, had he continued to allow fear to prevent him from following God's call to liberate the children of Israel. Here is Peter, denying his lord and master, giving in to fear, despairing and alone. Here is where you or I could be suspicious of anyone who enters our place of worship who doesn't look like us. It could consume us for the entire service (or an entire movie, in Steve Neumann's case) as we think of all the worst-case scenarios and evil that could happen and how we would react. It could force us to leave church or temple early, head directly to our car, and seek safety alone at home, all the while completely missing out on our intended time for prayer and worship.

In reflecting on what brings us fear, we must be willing to examine our own unconscious biases. In 1995 I spent a year interning in the newsroom at Austin's ABC station. I was preparing for a career in television news and was eager to get real world experience. At the time, the department was being led by news director Carole Kneeland. Kneeland was making headlines nationally for her innovative approach to running a newsroom as well as how the news was gathered and reported. First, Kneeland pulled back from reporting on every crime that happened in the city, instead imposing guidelines for what made it on the evening news. With that, suspect descriptions could no longer be as vague as "a Black male about five feet, eleven inches, in his thirties." How many thousands of Black males in the city fit that description? Second, Kneeland tasked reporters with seeking out interviews and comments from people in the community with particular attention to diversity in age, race, and socioeconomic factors. Even the experts chosen for political and local commentary were held to this standard. While these guiding principles and awarenesses may not seem so novel more than twenty-five years later, at the time Kneeland was ahead of what would soon become a pivotal discovery in the study of unconscious, also called implicit, biases.

In 1998 a team of social psychologists from the University of Washington and Yale created a test they described as "a new tool that measures the unconscious roots of prejudice" which they estimated affects 90 to 95 percent of people.[13] What this means is subconsciously, often with no malice intended, many of us are more likely to interact with, hire, or even approach someone at a party who looks more like us. Around 2015, companies like Facebook, Google, and Yahoo began to realize that even though diverse recruitment efforts were strong, they still tended to hire mostly white and Asian men.[14] Additionally, they found that if hired, minority individuals were less likely to stay with the company and thrive. Research revealed that professional traits like working in a group, solving problems, and social interactions are all affected by our cultural background and experiences.

While the hiring process had been adapted to include more diversity, the culture of these companies remained the same and often didn't take into account the many different ways of interacting, learning, and expressing oneself that were housed under one roof. Why do these biases exist in all of us, especially if they aren't meant with malice? Social scientists describe it as in-group and out-group differentiations that help us make our way in the world. According to an article by Hannah Devlin in the *Guardian*, "Scientists believe that stereotypes in general serve a purpose because clustering people into groups with expected traits help us navigate the world without being overwhelmed by information. The downside is that the potential for prejudice is hardwired into human cognition."[15] Likewise, philosopher Kwame Anthony Appiah notes that human beings assume identities because it makes it possible to know where we fit socially and helps us to understand hierarchies, dominance, and subordination.[16] Therefore it should come as no surprise that our unconscious biases affect what instigates fear in each of us.

What unconscious biases do you have because of your personal experiences or the news you consume? No one needs it pointed out that white males have committed the majority of mass shootings in our country. Yet before the insurrection at the Capitol, I don't think most white people would have pinpointed a middle-aged white man as the one who causes the highest level of concern. Post–September 11, former archbishop of Canterbury Rowan Williams compared the feelings many Americans had after the 9/11 attacks to the feelings following the Oklahoma City bombing. One event was carried out by Muslim extremists and the other was perpetrated by Timothy McVeigh, a white former US soldier who fought in the Gulf War.

> The USA was shocked by the Oklahoma bombing, yet curiously, this internal assault did not make people afraid in the same way. It is almost as if an act of brutal violence from within, as it were, can be assimilated by the imagination as this [the attacks on September 11] cannot.[17]

For as long as we all can remember, we've been taught or at least understood that white men are the "in group" atop the hierarchy. It was much harder for many Americans to feel as threatened by McVeigh as they would have been (and later were) had the attack been an international terrorist incident. Being aware of our biases is important in understanding our fear and taking a more rational look at the reality of its accuracy.

Denying and Normalizing Fear

"I grew up in a war zone, and in a war zone there are a lot of experiences that justify a lot of fear,"[18] my friend Irit Umani told me as we settled in for a conversation on a rainy January morning. I always enjoy my time with Umani because I find her warm, inspiring, and always authentic. I also think she is wise—the kind of wisdom that comes from living a full and spiritual life beginning in her birthplace of Haifa, Israel, to living at the Lama Foundation, an intentional spiritual community in New Mexico, to her present-day home in Austin, Texas. As we began our conversation, Umani recalled a time in the early 1990s when the Israeli government issued gas masks to its citizens during the Gulf War. People were told to carry the masks with them to and from places so they could use them at a moment's notice. She painted hers with peace signs and went about life. When the warnings were strong enough to warrant an in-shelter lockdown, Umani sealed off an inner safe room in her home and listened as bombs were intercepted in the distance. "In order to live for years in a war zone and still have a life, the whole society lives in somewhat of an awareness or acute awareness and on the very other side of it in total denial," she explained. "So you normalize it. It's a psychological protection that we put on that is a survival mechanism because if we didn't do that we'd go crazy because someone is attempting to kill us."[19]

Psychologists and mental health experts both praise and warn about the various states of denial. According to the Mayo Clinic, "Refusing to face facts might seem unhealthy. Sometimes, though, a short period of denial can be helpful. Being in denial gives your mind the opportunity to unconsciously absorb shocking or distressing information at a pace that won't send you into a psychological tailspin."[20] The Psalms demonstrate the human psyche properly acknowledging fear and uncertainty; the psalmists are often speaking of the threats and the enemies that menace them, as in Psalm 22:

I am poured out like water,
>   and all my bones are out of joint;
>   my heart is like wax;
> it is melted within my breast;
>   my mouth is dried up like a potsherd,
>   and my tongue sticks to my jaws;
> you lay me in the dust of death.
>   For dogs are all around me;
> a company of evildoers encircles me.[21]

In seeking that proper balance between fear and faith, the psalmists acknowledge the dangers of this life so that they can then pray
for God's intervention. While the psychological protection of denial
may serve us well for a while, I describe it as a "protect now, pay
later" coping mechanism. Before we can properly seek a solution, we
have to eventually admit the problem.

After many years of living in the United States, Umani went
to visit her daughter in Kfar Saba, located on the outskirts of Tel
Aviv. As they prepared to celebrate Shabbat, the sirens sounded outside. Everyone was ushered into the safe room as usual; however,
Umani—who was no longer accustomed to normalizing the fear—
admitted to getting "a bit hysterical."

> Only when you live in this constantly can you call
> this normal and go about your business. Then you
> leave, and that's when it's safe to start feeling the
> post-traumatic stress and call insane "insane." You
> put on the shield until it's safe to take it off. Once
> you take it off you aren't as protected emotion-
> ally. . . . The mind-blowing thing to me was, we
> then went back to the living room and resumed the
> Shabbat celebration and meal as if what just had
> happened hadn't happened at all.[22]

Denying reality (for instance, denying that mass shootings do
occasionally happen at places of worship) might prevent a church
from assessing what reasonable measures could be put in place to

lower the likelihood of a shooting or reduce mass injuries and causalities if one did occur. When I see people struggle with the decision whether to do the work involved in implementing a security plan, I simply ask, "Are you comfortable with what you have now in terms of security and safety?" Almost always the answer is "no": they feel like it could be better. This acknowledgement provides the first small step in their work to move forward.

To offer some perspective in assessing the level of "appropriate" fear, I wanted to know when church shootings went from being an anomaly that we could rightly dismiss as a one-time act to the trend we have experienced in recent decades. Here's what I found. The first modern-day mass shooting at a church happened at the First Baptist Church in Daingerfield, Texas. On June 22, 1980, former high school teacher Alvin Lee King III killed five people and wounded ten others after opening fire on the congregation during a Sunday service. King was armed with several guns and was angry that church members had declined to testify on his behalf at an upcoming trial in which he was accused of rape. Three hundred members were in the congregation, with many more listening via a live radio broadcast.[23] The next shooting didn't happen for eleven years. On August 9, 1991, six monks, a nun, and two others were shot execution-style during a robbery at the Waddell Buddhist Temple in Arizona.[24] The next shooting at a place of worship wasn't until 1999 at Wedgewood Baptist Church in Ft. Worth, Texas. That's only three shootings in nineteen years. However, in 2001 we started to see a steady uptick in the number of mass shootings at our sacred places that continued until the COVID-19 pandemic hit in 2020 and many churches closed their doors.[25] That's what it took to stop the trend, at least for the time being. While unhealthy fear can cause us to take action we might not otherwise take, or rationalize something that goes against our core beliefs, denying the fear can prolong our anxiety and simply waste time we could spend working to reduce these incidents.

Instinct and Healthy Fear

Many years ago, I read *The Gift of Fear* by Gavin de Becker. He took his teaching of fear and intuition to a national audience during a 1997 appearance on the *Oprah Winfrey Show*. His message to millions of viewers: good, healthy fear is a gift we all harbor; when we tap into it, it can save us. In his book, de Becker tells the story of airline pilot Robert Thompson, who described the time he walked into a convenience store and was immediately overcome by an overwhelming sense of fear. It was so strong that he turned around and darted out.

> Well, now that I think back, the guy behind the counter looked at me with a very rapid glance, just jerked his head toward me for an instant, and I guess I'm used to the clerk sizing you up when you walk in, but he was intensely looking at another customer, and that must have seemed odd to me. I must have seen that he was concerned. I noticed that the clerk was focused on a customer who was wearing a big, heavy jacket, and of course, I now realize that it was hot, so that's probably where the guy was hiding the shotgun.[26]

Moments after Thompson left, a police officer entered the store and was shot and killed by the gunman. De Becker could only imagine that when the officer walked in, the clerk's face registered relief rather than the involuntary warning signal Thompson had so intensely felt from the clerk. De Becker explains that our intuition increases when we consciously or subconsciously perceive a risk. On heightened awareness, our brain processes everything much faster than our normal step-by-step rhythm and because it is all happening so quickly, we can't make sense of why we are suddenly, unexplainably afraid. Intuition, de Becker explains, "is knowing without knowing why."[27]

This feeling—what we often call our gut instinct—is less about fear and more about the perceived concern we have in that moment.

While fear extends to the future and what might happen, instinct is focused on the right now as we work to make sense of what we're seeing and what we should do next. How many times have we said, "I should have trusted my gut?" The distrust of our feeling comes in when we can't make sense of why we feel that way so we quickly start rationalizing that we are being too sensitive, too paranoid, or too fearful. This is a key training point for ushers and greeters in church security.

Ushers, greeters, and members of welcome committees are almost always the first people who see and talk with visitors. While many are trained, or at least told, to be aware if something doesn't seem right, many of them feel uncomfortable with making that assessment or speaking up if they notice something unusual. It's much easier to rationalize or compartmentalize it because no one wants to be suspicious and wrong, especially in a welcoming place of worship. However, I think one of the best conversations we can have is the difference between profiling or stereotyping and observing the facts that create reason for concern. Let's consider how we differentiate these.

Profiling and stereotyping are done out of our fear and biases, and often focus on the way a person looks: the color of their skin, their choice of clothing, or even the way they wear their hair. That's not to say someone wearing a trench coat on a hot summer day shouldn't catch our attention, but the defining characteristics of who they are shouldn't be what concerns us most. Observable facts, on the other hand, focus on a person's actions. When we greet them, do they seem like they are there to worship and curious about the service or small groups, or do they avoid eye contact and ask unusual or odd questions about the church's security measures? Perhaps they have a perfectly good reason to want to know what safety precautions are in place, but if that inner voice raises a red flag, the volunteer engaging them must have the training, confidence, and permission to share that concern. Equally important, a place of worship must have a reporting system in place so a concern can immediately be dealt with and a closer look given to the situation.

As someone who was constantly being threatened with harm and violence, Dr. Martin Luther King Jr, described fear as a psychological necessity that propels us forward. "Normal fear motivates us to improve our individual and collective welfare; abnormal fear constantly poisons and distorts our inner lives. Our problem is not to be rid of fear but rather to harness and master it."[28] In seeking the proper balance between faith and fear, we are seeking not to be overwhelmed by fear, but to allow our faith to work within that space. Yes, the world is full of dangers and difficulties, but as the Psalms remind us, God accompanies us in them. David wrote in Psalm 27:1, "The LORD is my light and my salvation; whom shall I fear? The LORD is the stronghold of my life; of whom shall I be afraid?" In a world full of things to fear, this is important wisdom. In harnessing our fear, we resist the urge to be frightened away from church on a Sunday morning. Likewise, we also refuse to be overcome by fear, and we create a fortress where only those known to us are allowed to comfortably enter. Instead, my hope is houses of worship will work to develop a safety plan that comes not from a place of fear, but out of the duty to create measured and planned responses aimed at reducing the knee-jerk reactions, anxiety, and confusion that normally happens in a quickly unfolding situation. To do this, we must draw on our courage to sit in the hard conversations and have honest dialogue about how we best feel committed and called to making our sacred spaces safer for everyone.

CHAPTER 2

Guns in Sacred Spaces

L ike many people in the South, I grew up around guns and never thought much about it. Living in a small rural community, it was routine to see guns across racks in the back of pickup trucks and to accompany my stepdad to the shooting range on a Sunday afternoon (after church, of course). It wasn't until I had my first child that I insisted the guns in my own home be locked away. Eventually, with two toddlers in the house, I made the decision to own none at all. What changed? My perspective did. I now looked at providing safety and protection through a different lens.

We all have cultural, political, religious, and personal beliefs (and fears) that feed our feelings about guns, especially when it comes to having them in places as intimate as our homes and churches. Everyone on all sides of the issue feel they are right, and the politics connected to the conversation makes it even more divisive. What has become clear to me in the process of talking with church leaders and reading how faith communities are handling this issue is that there is no single correct answer. What might be right for a small rural church in Colorado with limited funds may be absolutely wrong for a church in the heart of lower Manhattan with ample resources. If we can enter into conversations that aren't centered on "right or wrong," but rather discuss what options best reflect *our* particular community's security needs, spiritual beliefs, and physical comfort level, our conversations will lead to a more clear and workable solution for our congregations. In an article discussing practical Christian pacifism in the *Christian Century*, David Hoekema sums it up nicely: "There is an urgent need for more open and honest discussion in the churches, for we are too quick to condemn those who bear witness in a way in which we do not feel called. We ought not to demand the same actions from everyone. Out of more open and honest discussion may come new and still untried ways of putting flesh on a shared vision of peace."[1] In this chapter, I will explore the ways places of worship are making decisions about firearms and some of the theology used during discernment.

Guns Not Allowed

Westmoreland Congregational United Church of Christ sits on a busy traffic circle in Bethesda, Maryland. The church is housed in an old building that dates back to 1948. It has four levels with nine entrances facing all different directions. When it came time to discuss an active shooter plan, senior minister Timothy Tutt says his congregation wasn't conflicted about *what* to do; they were conflicted about whether they wanted to do anything at all. Tutt and the Westmoreland congregation strongly believe they want an open church with unlocked doors. They want to assume the best of every person who walks inside. With this in mind, they don't allow guns on campus and declined hiring an off-duty officer who carries one. "The militarization of the church—for lack of a better term—doesn't seem to us to be consistent with the gospel of Jesus Christ," Tutt says. "A police officer in a uniform with or without a gun doesn't send the symbol that we are people who believe the peace makers are the blessed ones."[2] While many news stories have highlighted houses of worship increasing their number of armed officers on worship days, or even encouraging congregants to carry concealed handguns, Westmoreland Church isn't alone in its decision to forbid guns entirely. According to a 2019 survey of Protestant pastors, 27 percent say they have a no firearm policy for their campus.[3] When I asked where he draws the line between being an open and welcoming church and protecting those who come inside, Tutt tells me he believes if there is such a line, it's not drawn evenly down the middle; the line is drawn to weigh heavily on the side of welcoming everyone, even if that comes with increased risks. "I think a radical approach to theology, a radical approach to Jesus saying turn the other cheek, means you're forever putting yourself and the people you love at risk," Tutt says. "That's just simply a part of doing your best to live out the gospel."[4]

Jesus speaking of turning the other cheek in response to violence may or may not be a useful way of thinking about church safety. Many believe the passage is not to be taken literally as offering oneself up to violence but to be thought of as a way to assert strength against a violent oppressor. Theologian and activist Walter Wink wrote, "By turning the cheek then, the inferior party is saying 'I'm not inferior to you. I'm a human being. I refuse to be humiliated any longer. I am your equal. I'm a child of God. I won't take it anymore.'"[5] In the Gospel of Matthew, the Sermon on the Mount is the central ethical teaching of Jesus, and it includes a number of statements about being persecuted, being meek, being mourners, and being pure in heart, none of which, again, seem to invite Christians to take up arms to protect themselves. In fact, Jesus says that those who seek to be peacemakers—and those who are reviled and persecuted—are actually blessed:

> Blessed are the peacemakers, for they will be called children of God.
> Blessed are those who are persecuted for righteousness; sake, for theirs is the kingdom of heaven.
> . . . Rejoice and be glad, for your reward is great in heaven, for in the same way they persecuted the prophets who were before you.[6]

The decision on whether to make a security plan wasn't the first time Tutt had to weigh the options of personal safety in the church. In the summer of 2011, he was the senior pastor at United Christian Church in Austin, Texas. For no reason he or police could figure, someone started shooting at the church in the middle of the night. Over time, the shots started coming earlier in the evening, ultimately happening when the choir was in the building. "The fear in the congregation was palpable over those weeks," Tutt said. Feelings ranged from people not wanting to come to church to people wanting to cancel evening programs. "But for me, what we do as a church is proclaim the good news of Jesus Christ and love in grace and kindness and affirmation to all people so I'm going to stand here and do this because that's my job. Was I afraid on those Sundays? Yeah."[7] The gunfire finally ended when police found that a man who lived near the church was responsible, although a motive was never established. While many churches and pastors, hold steadfast that their place of worship is a gun-free area despite the risks, more and more are reconsidering their thoughts when it comes to hiring off-duty officers, many of whom are required to carry a gun as part of their uniform.

Armed Off-Duty Officers

The Rev. Dr. Chuck Treadwell is the rector of my beloved St. David's Episcopal Church in Austin. Not only is St. David's my home church, it was my place of employment for ten years and where I began my work on church security. Having worked with Treadwell for many years, I know the issues he wrestled with when it came to our initial security planning. I asked him if we could talk about those things with the benefit of hindsight guiding the discussion. As we began, Treadwell reminded me of an incident in 2016 that occurred as he was setting the altar for communion during a Sunday morning service. A man—who appeared somewhat disoriented—made his way from the back of the church up the center aisle. "The choir *parted* and let him through!" Treadwell laughed, thinking back. The man walked up to the altar, moved inside the rail, and stood next to him before Treadwell even realized he was there. Treadwell's wife watched in fear from a church pew. "He just asked for a blessing, which I gave him, then he turned around and left."⁸ The incident wasn't what prompted St. David's to hire its first security guard, but it did emphasize some of the safety concerns the downtown church had long faced. St. David's sits one block north of the city's famed entertainment district, Sixth Street, and right next to the Austin Resource Center for the Homeless (ARCH), which provides services and shelter to hundreds of Austin's homeless population. While some are valued members of the parish and never cause reasons for concern, problems began surfacing when a few visitors experiencing homelessness started panhandling inside and outside the church on Sundays. That, coupled with several verbal outbursts, concerned the staff and parish administrator enough to hire a local security company to provide an unarmed guard on Sunday mornings. It was a good solution and worked well. However, a few months later a rash of car break-ins in the church garage called for increased security in the way of an off-duty officer.

"We didn't make a decision to hire an armed officer; that was not the driving factor that he was armed," Treadwell said. "We made a decision to hire an off-duty police officer because they could take someone into custody [for the car break-ins]." St. David's decision reflects the position in which many churches find themselves: the need for police presence to deter criminal activity with the added bonus of being able to immediately detain or arrest someone caught in the act. Treadwell didn't hide the fact there was pushback. People didn't like the optics of seeing a police officer with a gun, especially in a house of worship that was clearly marked as a gun-free campus banning concealed carry guns. The clergy were all in agreement: church is no place for guns. "We come to worship God open-hearted and empty-handed (as far as guns)," Treadwell said. Furthermore, the particular environment of St. David's—a downtown church surrounded by transient and refugee neighbors—has a definite theological context. The Bible speaks often about the poor, the widow, the orphan, and the alien, and Jesus speaks specifically about "the least of these" in Matthew 25, where he discusses the ethical behavior required of Christians, including welcoming the stranger in his name: "Truly I tell you, just as you did it to one of the least of these who are members of my family, you did it to me."[9]

So how did Treadwell come to a final decision on an armed off-duty officer? In his discernment he took three things into consideration: (1) the optics of an armed officer, (2) the contradictory theology of weapons in the building, and (3) who may *not* come into the church because of the officer's presence (with particular attention to Austin considering itself a sanctuary city).[10] Ultimately, he decided the three arguments and concerns were less compelling than the church's regular and ongoing need to de-escalate situations, handle disruptions, and deter theft. "We find ourselves at that intersection of a theology of peace and a theology of compassion, patience, and turning the other cheek in countering the realities of the world that are often dangerous and the person who wants to hurt you does not share that theology. I do feel that occasionally we have to fight back to protect the innocent, but how we do that matters a lot."[11]

Christianity, as we will see, does have a just war tradition that argues that protection of the innocent is of value, but this decision also depends, as Treadwell suggests, on many variables. Following the 2019 Poway synagogue shooting in California, Rabbi Devorah Marcus from Temple Emanu-El of San Diego appeared on PBS News Hour with Judy Woodruff to discuss the synagogue's decision to elevate security following this incident.

> In the end, we made that choice to move to armed guards for a number of different reasons. One, as was demonstrated at Chabad, first of all, it decreases the appearance of being a soft target, and people who come in to do these attacks often flee immediately when they are confronted with other people who are armed and trained. So, we didn't do this because we glorify violence or we celebrate guns. We're very much not in favor of a violent culture. We made the transition to switch to armed guards because we felt that it was the best way to keep everyone in our community safe.[12]

Wilshire Baptist Church in Dallas reevaluates its security measures regularly, especially following a nearby shooting in 2019 and, prior to that, the 2017 shooting in Sutherland Springs, Texas. In an email sent to church members in January 2020, senior pastor George Mason explained the church's decision to utilize armed security guards while also remaining faithful followers of God.

> I want to call attention to a distinction I weigh in my own mind spiritually between safety and security. Safety procedures are wise and practical. When we love one another, we want to protect each other from potential accidents and maliciously minded intruders. . . . Security involves a higher level of protection than safety, both practically and philosophically. Being a church, we want to live in a way that promotes our values of welcoming strangers, loving our neighbors, and practicing nonviolent ways of living. We are a peaceable people, and we want to internalize our understanding that true security is found only in God. We will never be completely secure in this life, no matter our defensive preparations. We do not want our church to become an armed fortress or for a spirit of fear to become pervasive among us.[13]

Like the Rev. Tutt in Maryland, Mason acknowledged the tensions of welcoming the stranger and protecting the flock and expressed his hopes that Wilshire Baptist would choose hospitality as a primary value. Rather than live in fear, both pastors want to lean into the belief that God is working in all that happens. This is not a belief that God will intervene to protect worshippers; it is a belief that God is present in good times and bad, and that living up to the highest calling of our faith is an essential witness, even in the face of fear and violence.

I've talked with plenty of church leaders who have struggled with the decision to hire an armed officer and eventually conclude it is the best thing for their community. At that point what I see most often is guidelines put in place with parameters on where police presence is expected and where it is allowed in emergency-only situations in an effort to balance safety while still protecting the most sacred space of the church, the sanctuary, especially during worship. First United Methodist in Austin has written instructions that the officer will do routine patrol in and around the campus as well as assist with checking someone's bag if requested by clergy or someone in a leadership position. It specifically states the officer will not enter the sanctuary unless asked to do so or the officer deems there is a safety concern or threat. But, again, different spaces allow for different strategies.

Jim Shepherd is the former director of preservation of facilities at the Washington National Cathedral. I met Shepherd at a conference where we were on the same church safety panel and share a lot of the same approaches to security. He and I talked about the cathedral's long and impressive history of hosting presidential funerals and national services, including sermons given by Dr. King, Archbishop Desmond Tutu, and the Dalai Lama. Because of these ongoing high profile events in addition to the adjacent proximity of the three cathedral schools, an assessment was implemented by the Department of Homeland Security. The recommendations of this assessment led the cathedral and the schools to reassess their security measures and, ultimately, increase the size of its security program and create more location-specific control. This augmentation of security included designating a single point of entry for the weekdays and Saturday and adding armed officers inside the sanctuary on Sundays and during special events.

"They are directed to be quietly patrolling on the side aisles," Shepherd explained. "That initially got a lot of resistance, but we have the advantage of being such a large space. The building is large enough and the side aisles remote enough that you can have someone walking up and down those quietly during a service and 95 percent of people don't notice they are there."[14] During his time at the cathedral, Shepherd worked closely with the church's chief operating officer Rob Sokol. Sokol is now the chief administrative officer at Trinity Church Wall Street, where he oversees a massive multitiered security operation that watches over the church's two worship spaces and a twenty-six-story building that houses a new community center along with church and corporate offices. Like the National Cathedral, Trinity Church is considered a high-risk target as it sits mere blocks from the World Trade Center site and in Manhattan's financial district. Sokol will be the first to tell you that security comes at a real cost—financially and emotionally. His best advice for small, suburban, low-risk churches is to train staff and leadership on all aspects of emergency preparedness and only hire security to the extent you need it.

If security becomes your primary value above people and worship, then everything you do will be oriented around that value. To put too many resources and too much energy into deterring violence with armed guards strikes many as a betrayal of what they believe the gospel stands for. In Matthew 6 Jesus says, "Do not store up for yourselves treasures on earth, where moth and rust consume and where thieves break in and steal; but store up for yourselves treasures in heaven, where neither moth nor rust consumes and where thieves do not break in and steal. For where your treasure is, there your heart will be also."[15] This passage may be less about wealth and more about priorities and how you reflect and balance them.

Armed Church Security Teams

One of the most recent and well-known cases of an armed church security team stopping a gunman is the 2019 shooting at the West Freeway Church of Christ in White Settlement, Texas. Shooter Keith Kinnunen was known by those at the church since they had occasionally provided him with food, but he had become angry because they wouldn't also give him money.[16] On December 29, he entered the church wearing a fake beard, wig, and a long coat. He clearly caught the attention of the church's volunteer security team, which sat one team member behind him and adjusted a security camera to face him. During communion, Kinnunen left to use the bathroom and then stopped on the way back to his seat to talk with Tony Wallace, who was standing at the back of the church. Video from the security camera shows Kinnunen pulling a shotgun out from under his coat and shooting Wallace and another member of the security team, Richard White. As Kinnunen turned the gun toward the front of the church, security team member Jack Wilson shot him; he went down immediately. The whole scenario played out in six seconds over the church's livestream video feed.[17]

Those in favor of armed church members and armed church security teams praised Wilson's actions as the perfect example of the "good guy with a gun" argument. Texas governor Greg Abbott declared Wilson a hero and awarded him the state's highest civilian award, the Governor's Medal of Courage.[18] We learned that not only did Wilson have a license to carry a handgun, he once owned a firearms training academy, where he was an instructor and served his community as a reserve deputy. I can't think of anyone more qualified to be on a church security team, and he was widely praised for preventing what surely would have been more deaths.[19] Following the incident, religious leaders scrambled to address parishioner concerns about having guns in their worship space. In the 2019 survey of Protestant pastors mentioned earlier, 45 percent of the pastors surveyed report their security measures include armed church members. The tendency to have armed members appears, at least on the surface, to be in relation to the denomination. Pastors in Pentecostal (71 percent), Baptist (65 percent), and Church of Christ (53 percent) denominations were more likely to have armed members compared to pastors in Methodist (32 percent), Lutheran (27 percent), and Presbyterian or Reformed (27 percent) denominations who answered the survey. One of the few books on church security, *Defending the Flock* by Kris, P. Moloney, an author with a military and police background, quotes 1 Peter on the necessity of being aware and prepared: "Be of sober spirit, be on the alert. Your adversary, the devil, prowls around like a roaring lion, seeking someone to devour. So resist him, firm in your faith, knowing that the same experiences of suffering are being accomplished by your brothers and sisters who are in the world."[20] Advocates of guns in the pews also cite Nehemiah 4:14b as support of the use of force to protect those we love: "Remember the

LORD, who is great and awesome, and fight for your kin, your sons, your daughters, your wives, and your homes."

Ted Elmore is the prayer and special projects strategist with the Southern Baptists of Texas Convention and served as a pastor of First Baptist in Franklin, Texas. As part of the panel discussion with Judy Woodruff on PBS, Elmore told the audience that First Baptist has a security team made up of current and former law enforcement officers in addition to other safety precautions such as cameras, locked doors, and routine patrols. Elmore said prayer was part of their response as they sought the protection of God but appropriate measures had to be taken. "It is my responsibility and our responsibility, as leaders in the faith community, to protect our flock from the wolves, and there's no greater wolf than an assassin. And so we take prudent measures to protect our children, to protect our elderly, praying every moment that those measures of neutralizing a shooter never have to happen."21

The image of the shepherd protecting his flock is found in both the Old and New Testaments. In discussing this scripture, Rabbi Hillel Norry told CNN, "If we're the shepherds, the first job of the shepherd is to protect the flock from the wolf. . . . Why does a shepherd carry a stick? So he can whack the wolf."22 A similar image occurs again in the New Testament, that of the good shepherd who takes responsibility for his flock.

> I am the good shepherd. The good shepherd lays down his life for the sheep. The hired hand, who is not the shepherd and does not own the sheep, sees the wolf coming and leaves the sheep and runs away—and the wolf snatches them and scatters them. The hired hand runs away because a hired hand does not care for the sheep. I am the good shepherd. I know my own and my own know me, just as the Father knows me and I know the Father. And I lay down my life for the sheep."23

Based on such readings, one can see how a pastor—a word actually drawn from the Latin word for "shepherd"—feels called to keep their flock safe.

While theology often plays a role in a decision to arm church and security team members, sometimes it simply comes down to financial resources. The Joyful Heart Church sits just ten miles down the road from where the Sutherland Springs Baptist Church shooting took place. They too are a small congregation in a rural part of Texas. Following the Sutherland Springs attack, the Joyful Heart husband and wife pastor team increased security by adding surveillance cameras and hiring private security officers. They also made the decision to allow church members to arm themselves as a way of increasing protection at no additional financial cost. This decision isn't uncommon as more state legislatures have made it easier for people to carry guns in houses of worship.[24] Pastor Moore, who sat at lunch with the parishioner who was terrified of a shooting at church, said his perspective on congregants "packing" a gun has evolved over the years. As a senior pastor at Central Presbyterian in Austin, he testified against Texas House bill 308 in March 2015. The bill expanded places where licensed handgun owners can carry a gun, and he actively opposed it. Moore remembers, "Even at a liberal church in the state of Texas, this was not going to be without controversy." And it wasn't. One whom Moore described as "a beloved member" of the church's governing board was upset with him for considering putting up *No Guns Allowed* signs at entrances to the church. She recited talking points from the National Rifle Association (NRA) and declared that her spouse might never come to the church again, which Moore realized was really the heart of the matter. Several months later Moore accepted the call as pastor at Buckhorn Presbyterian Church in Colorado. It was a smaller, more conservative congregation. He learned there, and later in his role as a security consultant for the region, that people—especially those in rural areas—have a different relationship with guns and local law enforcement than those in larger, more metropolitan places. While Moore's top focus remained safety training, he also came to see that there are some places of worship where having one or two people who are trained and experienced in carrying and using firearms can be an appropriate and responsible decision. Moore said it was a conversation with a rabbi friend of his who "opened my eyes to the blanket restriction on guns might not be the only faithful way to move forward." Moore remembered:

> He was born in the Ukraine and I imagine he knew personally and historically what it was like to be a persecuted religious minority. For his grandparents the question of protecting houses of worship was literally a life or death issue. He struck me a deeply faithful person and the calm way in which he said what he said about guns in houses of worship simply made me question my own visceral opposition to that sort of thing. I'm not sure it changed my mind . . . but it did highlight the truth that faithful people can come to different conclusions. We have different lived experiences and his lived experience was one that was particularly difficult for me ignore.

Moore said after a while in his new role, he realized he couldn't change the culture about guns, but he was able to balance it with additional conversations about safety, including suggesting fire drills to help better identify safe ways to exit the building if needed. "You can't talk about church safety if you only talk about guns."25

Like Pastor Moore, what I've come to see in the debate over guns is that every house of worship offers first and foremost a faithful prayer for peace. While each place will have to determine what is best for its community, it will also have to determine what is best for our times. What does armed security look and feel like in the wake of the Black Lives Matter movement and conversations around defunding the police? Did the attack on the US Capitol change our perspective on how and why we secure sacred places? Our current events directly impact how safe we feel in our places of worship, as does our proximity to a past shooting or having been the target of one. All of these factors should be part of our thought process as we move forward. As the familiar passage from Ecclesiastes reminds us:

> To every thing there is a season, and a time to every purpose under the heaven:
> A time to be born, and a time to die; a time to plant, and a time to pluck up that which is planted;
> A time to kill, and a time to heal; a time to break down, and a time to build up;
> A time to weep, and a time to laugh; a time to mourn, and a time to dance;
> A time to cast away stones, and a time to gather stones together; a time to embrace, and a time to refrain from embracing;
> A time to get, and a time to lose; a time to keep, and a time to cast away;
> A time to rend, and a time to sew; a time to keep silence, and a time to speak;
> A time to love, and a time to hate; a time of war, and a time of peace.[26]

CHAPTER 3

Faith, Courage, and Mass Tragedy

Psalm 23

The LORD is my shepherd, I shall not want.
 2 He makes me lie down in green pastures;
he leads me beside still waters;
  3 he restores my soul.
He leads me in right paths
  for his name's sake.
 4 Even though I walk through the darkest valley,
  I fear no evil;
for you are with me;
  your rod and your staff—
  they comfort me.
 5 You prepare a table before me
  in the presence of my enemies;
you anoint my head with oil;
  my cup overflows.
 6 Surely goodness and mercy shall follow me
  all the days of my life,
and I shall dwell in the house of the LORD
  my whole life long.

It's undoubtedly one of the best-known and most-used of all the psalms. In the Revised Common Lectionary, the selection of scripture employed by a majority of American Christians in their Sunday worship, Psalm 23 appears multiple times during the year. It is part of the readings in the Episcopal Book of Common Prayer for the services around the major liturgical events of our lives: Holy Baptism, Ministration to the Sick, Thanksgiving for a Birth or Adoption, and Burial of the Dead. It is no surprise then that Mother Emanuel's pastor, the Rev. Eric Manning, chose to read this life-marking psalm when he was asked to speak at the funeral of ninety-seven-year-old Rose Mallinger, the oldest victim of the Tree of Life synagogue shooting in Pittsburgh.[1] As mourners gathered, Rev. Manning offered words of comfort, just as the Mother Emanuel community had been comforted three years earlier.

Why is Psalm 23 so useful? What is it about this psalm that brings us a sense of peace, especially in the midst of powerful tragedy? Because when we sit with what has happened and still struggle to find the will to get out of bed, pray for the hurt, or attend yet another rally, Psalm 23 offers us a way. It's not the promise of safety nor the promise of an easy life. It's not the promise that God will step in and circumvent evil from happening. Rather, it's the promise that no matter what happens, God is there on the journey with us, whether we're resting in green pastures or trudging through the deepest, darkest valley we have ever known. Survivors and family members of those who were killed at Mother Emanuel offered a glimpse of what faith and courage looked like in the most trying of times, but they also knew the road through the valley wasn't an easy one to find or follow.

After the tragic shooting in Charleston, Mother Emanuel could have closed its doors. No one would have blamed them for taking weeks or months to grieve, repair damage, and find their new normal. But that is not what they chose. The church opened its doors just four days after the shooting. They cleared memorial flowers from the walkway and welcomed an overflowing Sunday crowd for the first worship service after nine of their own, including head pastor Clementa Pinckney, had been killed. With Pinckney's chair draped in black cloth, the choir sang the beloved hymn "Blessed Assurance":

Perfect submission, all is at rest
I in my Savior am happy and blessed
Watching and waiting, looking above
Filled with His goodness, lost in His love

This is my story, this is my song
Praising my Savior all the day long
This is my story, this is my song
Praising my Savior all the day long.[2]

The Rev. Norvell Goff, presiding elder of the Edisto District
of the State Conference of the AME Church, stood up to preach.
"The doors of the church are open, praise be to God. No evildoer,
no demon in hell or on Earth can close the doors of God's church."[3]

During this sermon, the Rev. Sharon Risher was still trying
to accept the reality that her mother, eighty-year-old Ethel Lance,
had been one of the people gunned down. Lance had attended
the historic Black church since 1974 and had served in many roles,
including that of usher. Distinguished by its black or white uniform
(depending on the occasion) and its signature white gloves, Lance
was always proud of the role. At the time of her death, she was also
a sexton for the church she had helped keep clean for decades. As
Risher notes in *For Such a Time as This: Hope and Forgiveness
after the Charleston Massacre,* if the church was open, her mom
was there. That fact made the initial news that a shooting had taken
place at the church even more devastating. Risher knew without a
doubt her mom faithfully attended Wednesday night Bible study, as
did several of her relatives. All Risher could do was hope and pray
that her mom somehow managed to escape the gunfire, or at least
survive it. Hours later and hundreds of miles away from Charleston,
Risher recalls letting out a guttural scream upon learning her mom
was one of the dead. "I was in that abyss that we sing about so often
in the Black Church. That time when you're poignantly aware that
you have nobody but Jesus to talk to."[4] As a hospital chaplain in
Dallas, Risher was trained in dealing with death and tragedy but
nothing had prepared her for this type of loss. She spent days pulling
herself together to make the trip home where she would gather with

her siblings and bury their mother. Not only had Risher lost her mom, but two cousins and her childhood friend Myra Thompson, who was leading Bible study for the first time, had also been killed. Risher was intimately connected to four of what became known as the Emmanuel Nine.

Nine days after the shooting, President Barack Obama gave the eulogy for the church's beloved Rev. Pinckney, who had been seated next to the gunman when the attack began. "The Bible calls us to hope. To persevere, and have faith in things not seen," Obama said. "They were still living by faith when they died, scripture tells us. They did not receive the things promised; they only saw them and welcomed them from a distance, admitting that they were foreigners and strangers on Earth."[5] By calling on Americans to continue to hope, to continue to persevere, and to continue to have faith, Obama offered a way to try and deal with such overwhelming and senseless tragedy. Why is our faith so often challenged when we need it the most? Former archbishop Rowan Williams spoke to this following the September 11 attacks. Williams unexpectedly found himself in the midst of 9/11 just blocks away from the World Trade Center buildings when the planes struck on that fateful day. With air travel shut down, there was nowhere to go; he couldn't leave for his home in Wales had he wanted to. Instead, he grappled with the aftermath, trying to understand and model how to faithfully respond to violence and fear.

> The morning after [September 11], very early, I was stopped in the street in New York by a youngish man who turned out to be an airline pilot and Catholic. He wanted to know what the hell God was doing when the planes hit the towers. What do you say? The usual fumbling about how God doesn't intervene, which sounds like a lame apology for some kind of "policy" on God's part, a policy exposed as heartless in the face of such suffering? Something about how God is there in the sacrificial work of the rescuers, in the risks they take? I

tried saying bits of this, but there was no clearer answer than there ever is. Any really outrageous human action tests to the limit our careful theological principles about God's refusal to interfere with created freedom. That God has made a world in which he doesn't casually step in to solve problems is fairly central to a lot of Christian faith. He has made the world so that evil forces can't be frustrated or aborted (where would he stop, for goodness sake? he'd have to be intervening every instant of human history) but have to be confronted, suffered, taken forward, healed in the complex process of human history, always in collaboration with what we do and say and pray. I do believe that; but I don't think you can *say* it with much conviction outside the context of people actually doing the action and the prayer. In the street that morning, all I had was words. I wasn't surprised they didn't help. He was a lifelong Christian believer, but for the first time it came home to him that he might be committed to a God who could seem useless in a crisis.[6]

It's hard to imagine a world where God is useless, although in that very moment it may certainly feel so. However, within hours of the planes crashing, people across the world poured into churches, mosques, and synagogues; in the days that followed, attendance soared in places of worship. Yes, maybe some people were angry at God, but they didn't show up to proclaim that. Instead, we asked God to stand with us in the mess and tragedy. We asked God for healing and a safer world. We prayed. We kept the faith and continued to preach, teach, and live the gospel. Washington National Cathedral's canon theologian Kelly Brown Douglas called on the same unwavering faith following the not guilty verdict in the 2012 shooting death of Trayvon Martin, which came in on a Saturday night with Douglas scheduled to preach the following morning.

She had to make room for the injustice. "Prior to the service a time was set aside for people to express their feelings about the verdict," Brown wrote in *Stand Your Ground: Black Bodies and the Justice of God*. "Many people spoke through their tears as they expressed their sadness, disappointment, fears, and incredulity. . . . There was an overall sense of anger and frustration. But what struck me the most in all the testimonies was that no one lashed out at God. No one doubted God. No one blamed God."[7]

The question of where God is in the face of evil—a field of religious reasoning called *theodicy*—is a core problem for many different faiths. If God is all-powerful, good, and just, then why is there evil in the world? Why, for example, did millions of Jews perish in the Holocaust? Why was Dylann Roof "allowed" to kill nine faithful people during prayer? The "problem of evil," as it is sometimes put, causes many to question their faith in God—and their understanding of God—but it can also lead to a more robust understanding of God and of God's world. Evil, tragedy, and death have been part of the human story since the very beginning, and it is essential that we find a story that can hold a place for God and for the reality of suffering at the same time.

Holocaust survivor Elie Wiesel was in Auschwitz with his father when he was a teenager. In the book *Night*, he recounts how he witnessed numerous instances of religious doubt prompted by tremendous injustice and human suffering, including his memory of a rabbi from Poland:

> He was always praying, in the block, at work, in ranks. He recited entire pages from the Talmud, arguing with himself, asking and answering himself endless questions. One day he said to me: "It's over. God is no longer with us." The old rabbi encapsulated the argument about God's goodness and the presence of great evil: "I suffer hell in my soul and my flesh. I also have eyes, and I see what is being done here. Where is God's mercy? Where is

> God? How can I believe, how can anyone believe in
> this God of mercy?"[8]

In *Night*, Wiesel often expresses his own difficulty with continuing to love and serve a God who at times he felt had abandoned him to torture, humiliation, and murder in Auschwitz. "How," he wonders, "could I say to him: 'Blessed be Thou, Almighty, Master of the Universe, who chose us among all nations to be tortured day and night, to watch as our fathers, our mothers, our brothers end up in the furnaces?'"[9] After surviving to the tail end of the war, Wiesel was turned out of the camp and forced by the SS to march unceasingly to almost certain death. He found that "in spite of myself, a prayer formed inside me, a prayer to this God in whom I no longer believed."[10] And yet, despite this heartbreaking evidence of the rabbi's wrestling—and of his own—Wiesel often tells an Auschwitz story about witnessing three rabbis who put God on trial for permitting the suffering that surrounded them. They submitted the evidence against God, weighed it, and found God guilty. And then, Wiesel says, they went to offer evening prayer to that God they had just accused of indifference. "At the end of the trial, they used the word *chayav* rather than 'guilty,'" Wiesel clarified in 2008 in response to some who questioned whether the incident had actually happened. "It means 'He owes us something.' Then we went to pray."[11] In the face of one of the greatest atrocities in history, faithful people accepted the real difficulties of believing in a God of love in a world filled with pain—and chose to go on believing.

Different explanations of the relationship between God and evil can help us be courageous in faith. As Williams noted, a central element of faith for many Christians is that God doesn't simply step in to stop things, even if we may believe God could do so. Other ways of thinking of God and God's relationship to the world may also help us step forward in continued faith. One of my favorite explanation comes from Scott Bader-Saye:

> I think a description of God's action in the world
> in which God just causes everything to happen—in

which every suffering, every atrocity is seen as God's
will—gives us a very skewed picture of what God is
like. And, biblically, it just doesn't hold together.
In Genesis 2 we have God saying, "Don't eat the
fruit of this tree," and then by Genesis 3 the human
beings are eating the fruit. Almost immediately we
have something happening that is not God's will.
All through scripture things happen that are not
God's will, and God manages somehow to continue
to pull God's people forward into the future God
wants for them.[12]

The image of God pulling us forward rather than pushing and
directing us from behind might be a powerful corrective for doubt
and fear. Sharon Risher has been praised for turning her grief
and pain into activism. She became what some call an "accidental
activist," because though no one chooses to be part of such pain
and heartache, some choose to be part of the change that can come
from it. I think of faith the same way Gavin de Becker describes
intuition, "knowing without knowing why."[13] If faith is the thing
that keeps our heads above water, our hearts open and our mind
intact—much like a lifeboat we desperately cling to—courage is
the movement that propels us forward through the valley, through
the grief, through the dark days. That movement might be our feet
kicking wildly below the surface or moving just barely enough to
cover ground. Nevertheless, we move in the direction of healing,
transformation, and continued believing. Martin Luther King
once preached that "courage is an inner resolution to go forward
in spite of obstacles and frightening solutions.[14] In his eulogy for
Pinckney, President Obama noted:

> The alleged killer could not imagine how the city
> of Charleston, under the good and wise leadership
> of Mayor Riley; how the state of South Carolina,
> how the United States of America would respond.
> Not merely with revulsion at his evil act, but with
> big-hearted generosity and, more importantly,

with a thoughtful introspection and self-examination that we so rarely see in public life.[15]

Obama went on to point out how faith isn't just what we have or what we feel inside; it's also the actions we do, and continue to do, for the greater good—the "imperative of a just society," as he calls it.[16] Obama then famously concluded the eulogy by singing the first few lines of "Amazing Grace." Those attending the service, especially the pastors seated behind him, were caught off guard; you can see it on their faces. They smiled. They gave witness. They stood with thousands of mourners in a filled-to-capacity arena and sang together. Despite the tragedy of the moment, God was present.

Moving Forward

One year after the shooting at Mother Emanuel, the church asked that people perform an act of kindness as "Acts of Amazing Grace Day" in memory of those who died. "With thousands of acts of grace being performed around the world, we will surely make the world a better place," the church posted on its Facebook page.[17] On the one-year anniversary of the Tree of Life shooting, city-wide community service projects were organized according to the Jewish imperative of doing good in the world. Rabbi Daniel Wasserman reflected on the anniversary, "We're not moving on. We're moving forward. There is a difference."[18] A full twenty years after the shooting at Wedgewood Baptist Church, members gathered to remember the seven who were killed and reflect on God's presence in the tragedy. "I think the opportunity that we have today is to declare God's faithfulness," said Jay Fannin, student pastor. "God was here twenty years ago. He's been with us, healing us and helping us—and walking with us all the way through this. And today is a celebration of that."[19] While finding the courage to move forward after a time of tragedy is difficult, maintaining our faith in a merciful God can likewise be challenging.

How often have we turned on the news and thought, "Not again, another church shooting"? It may not necessarily feel courageous three or four days later to dress for worship and drive to wherever that place is we bow our head and talk with God, but it is. The courage to keep showing up and living out our faith is something we choose to do in the midst of the chaos, fear, and heartbreak. That's not easy. Following her mother's funeral, Sharon Risher couldn't bear to go to church once back home in Dallas. "I didn't want to be around church people. I didn't want to be sitting in a church. I still believed, I just didn't feel connected. Even in the midst of reading scripture and listening to gospel music, there still was a kind of disconnect."[20] Instead, she turned to an online worship service that fed her in a way and in a space where she was comfortable receiving. Eighteen months later she summoned all the courage she had to attend Roof's federal trial. She wrote that the enormity of the trial was taxing. Like many of the victim's families from out of town, she was put up in a nearby hotel, and each day the families sat together at the courthouse. For Risher, the constant media barrage and requests for interviews were overwhelming, and each day was exhausting and emotionally draining. Then the next morning she would wake up and do it all over again. She said of the ordeal:

> We heard the terrible details of what had happened to our beloved. We saw the awful photos and every piece of evidence they had against this evil person. Lord, it was hard! But if someone got overwhelmed with emotion, someone nearby would place a comforting hand on that person's back or someone in the next seat would extend a hand. We formed such a bond. Nobody's family was more important than anyone else's. We were in this together.[21]

More than a year after Roof was found guilty and sentenced to death, Risher returned to Mother Emanuel for the first time. It was May 13, 2018, Mother's Day, and she preached from Psalm 119:71: "It was good for me to be afflicted so that I might learn your decrees." Some believe that hardship and suffering are our best teachers—that, paradoxically, they are a blessing and not a curse. But in another sense, the message running throughout Psalm 119 is how we need to embrace the ways of faith so that we can live happily and wisely. The Psalms in total argue that ongoing relationship with God is the key to human life and the only way to manage a world sometimes marked by despair. In their book *Out of the Depths*, Old Testament scholars Bernhard W. Anderson and Steven Bishop have called the Psalms "expressions of praise offered in a minor key in the confidence that Yahweh is faithful."[22] Certainly the Psalms do not minimize the ugly, the violent, or the terrifying elements of our reality. But they do remind us that even though we walk through the valley of the shadow of death, we need not fear evil, for God is with us. All that is required of us is the courage to go on walking.

CHAPTER 4

Our Duty to Protect

For the past year, the vast majority of American mosques, synagogues, and churches have remained closed due to the pandemic. As people of faith, we closed the doors because we didn't want to contribute to more people getting sick or, worse, dying. We wear masks, not just for ourselves, but for the safety of everyone: those we love and those we don't even know. Our duty, desire, and call to protect seems to be a basic human response shared by most of us, and we have found ways to balance safety with some semblance of normalcy. Creating a security plan is no different. Often I have heard people say they want to do more than "nothing" when it comes to church security planning, but at the same time they don't want to "go overboard." They know there's a middle ground, but they're not sure how to find it. We all struggle with the reality that being in a sacred place doesn't fully protect us in the way we hope it could, whether from violence or a virus. We wrestle with what we want our response to be and what it responsibly needs to be given today's world. As stated by the Rev. Chuck Treadwell, "We find ourselves at that intersection of a theology of peace and a theology of compassion and patience, and turning the other cheek, and countering the realities of the world, and the person who wants to hurt you does not share that theology."[1]

It's in Matthew 5:38–48 that Jesus admonishes us to turn the other cheek and go the second mile. Sometimes this lesson is taught

as a mix of fatalism and patience: the world is a difficult place, and
sometimes we are called to suffer faithfully as we take the punishment dished out by those who would harm us. However, in *Jesus and
Nonviolence: A Third Way*, Walter Wink argues that Jesus's com-
mandment to do these things is really about disarming someone's
superiority and control over us rather than meaning these literally.[2]
Wink goes on to explain that beyond fight or flight, there is a third
option Jesus gives us to respond. He offers more than a dozen examples, some of them listed below, of how to oppose evil without sub-
mitting to it or mirroring it.[3]

- Refuse to submit or to accept the inferior position.
- Take control of the power dynamic.
- Force the Powers to make decisions for which they are
  not prepared.
- Recognize your own power.
- Cause the oppressor to see you in a new light.

Granted, Wink is writing about wars, corrupt governments, and
civil unrest, but imagine incorporating some or all of these in your
security planning and training as nonviolent responses to an attack.
As Kelly Brown Douglas writes, "It is important to understand that
nonviolence is not the same as passivity or accommodation to violence. Rather, it is a forceful response that protects the integrity of
life. Violence seeks to do another harm, while nonviolence seeks to
rescue others from harm. It seeks to break the very cycle of violence
itself."[4] In "My Pilgrimage to Nonviolence," Martin Luther King
Jr. wrote at length about his discovery of the teachings of Mahatma
Gandhi and how these teachings of nonviolence were a turning
point for him:

> Gandhi was probably the first person in history to
> lift the love ethic of Jesus above mere interaction
> between individuals to a powerful and effective
> social force on a large scale. Love, for Gandhi, was a
> potent instrument for social and collective transfor-
> mation. It was in this Gandhian emphasis on love

and nonviolence that I discovered the method for social reform that I had been seeking for so many months. . . . My study of Gandhi convinced me that true pacifism is not nonresistance to evil, but non-violent resistance to evil. Between the two positions, there is a world of difference. Gandhi resisted evil with as much vigor and power as the violent resister, but he resisted with love instead of hate.[5]

I firmly believe that having a security plan that focuses on prevention rather than reaction reduces the likelihood violence will happen in your place of worship or will be needed to protect those you love. You should never create a plan out of fear or formulate one out of hate. Otherwise, we end up solely focused on the person or persons we believe will come in and do us harm and neglect the virtues and intentions with which we began. Instead, we have to love the people we are hoping to protect—which is everyone who comes through the door—more than we hate the person who wants to do harm. As Wink warns:

It means abandoning one of the greatest and oldest lies: that the world is made up of good people and bad people. There is a double movement of psychic energy. We identify someone else as evil and unconsciously project our own evil onto that person. But the person or system that we call enemy also evokes the evil within, like a piano string set vibrating by a piercing scream. This two-way traffic of projection and introjection, if not halted, eventually becomes a form of mimesis, where each party begins to imitate the other.[6]

Although Wink says it more eloquently and thoughtfully than I ever could, it comes down to not letting someone else's bad intentions change your good ones.

Christian Picciolini has made it his job to spread this message, and he does so having seen the worst that humans can do to each other.

He was fourteen years old when he was drawn into Hammerskin Nation, a white supremacist group that heavily relied on neo-Nazi rock music and bands to promote and spread its racist and violent ideology. In a TED Talk that has garnered more than four million views, Picciolini describes how he became one of the earliest and youngest leaders in America's most violent hate movement. As the son of hardworking immigrant parents, Picciolini recounts, he often found himself alone. One day he had a chance encounter with a man who tapped into his loneliness and promised him a place where he would belong. During this time, popular white power music was coming out of England, and it prompted Picciolini to organize America's first white power band, White American Youth. Through his lyrics, Picciolini preyed on the insecurities of young white males and promoted violence against those he deemed responsible for his problems. He blamed Black people for violence despite his own brutal acts. He blamed immigrants for suppressing his opportunities despite his own background.

> I stockpiled weapons for what I thought was an upcoming race war. I went to six high schools. I was kicked out of four of them, one of them twice. And twenty-five years ago, I wrote and performed racist music that found its way to the internet decades later and partially inspired a young white nationalist to walk into a sacred Charleston, South Carolina, church and senselessly massacre nine innocent people.[7]

After marrying and having his first child, Picciolini decided to physically distance himself from the Hammerskin Nation movement but found a way to support it from afar. He opened a record store in Chicago where he could sell white power music. To gain acceptance and somewhat legitimize his business in the community, he knew he needed to offer other kinds of music, so he included punk rock, heavy metal, and hip-hop albums. Customers of all kinds and colors started coming in: Jews, African Americans, and gays. Over time, Picciolini started having what he called "meaningful interactions" with them, despite the fact they knew he sold this other, vile music. His bad didn't change their good; quite the opposite:

> One day a young Black teen came in, and he was visibly upset. And I decided to ask him what was wrong. And he told me that his mother had been diagnosed with breast cancer. And suddenly, this young Black teenager, who I'd never had a meaningful conversation or interaction with, I was able to connect with because my own mother had been diagnosed with breast cancer, and I could feel his pain. On another occasion, a gay couple came in with their son, and it was undeniable to me that they loved their son in the same profound ways that I loved mine. And suddenly, I couldn't rationalize or justify the prejudice that I had in my head.[8]

Picciolini stopped stocking the white power music that accounted for 75 percent of his sales. After shuttering the store, he left the movement. The same music that had brought him in led him out, and he realized he could help others do the same. Partnering with other reformed white supremacists like Arno Michaelis, who spoke during the white supremacy hearings in DC, Picciolini cofounded Life After Hate, a nonprofit organization that has helped hundreds of others leave the movement.[9] His explanation of how he does this might be helpful as we think about our encounters with those who might come through our doors wanting to do us harm:

> And the way I do that is not by arguing with them, not by debating them, not by even telling them they're wrong, even though, boy, I want to sometimes. I don't do that. Instead, I don't push them away. I draw them in closer, and I listen very closely for their potholes, and then I begin to fill them in. I try to make people more resilient, more self-confident, more able to have skills to compete in the marketplace so that they don't have to blame

the other, the other that they've never met. Of all
the people I've worked with, they will all tell you the
same thing. One, they became extremists because
they wanted to belong, not because of ideology or
dogma. And second, what brought them out was
receiving compassion from the people they least
deserved it from, when they least deserved it.[10]

I want to be clear here: I'm not arguing that any amount of love
from those inside Mother Emanuel Church on June 17, 2015, would
or could have stopped Dylann Roof from taking the lives of innocent people. By that point, he had formulated a concrete plan. He
had made the ninety-minute drive from his home to the church on
at least six prior occasions to do reconnaissance; he was determined
to carry out an attack.[11] However, I do believe the way we protect
those we love must be grounded in our faithful desire to also love all
those, especially the marginalized, who enter our places of worship.

The Rt. Rev. Ian Douglas, Episcopal bishop in Connecticut and
a leader in Bishops United Against Gun Violence, expands on this
point: "The theological vocation of the church is not to be a fortress
against the world but rather is to be the place where the brokenness,
the alienation, and the hurt can be brought in and redeemed. That's
the theological starting point. That sounds nice, but if people don't
feel like they're safe in the pews, they're not going to even come in
and hear the gospel read." He goes on to remind us that the gospel
is not a story of being safe and sound. It's a story of death and dying
in service to a larger thing. We're called to risk everything for the
sake of the gospel, he says, but we still need to be smart about it.[12]
Being both smart and realistic about our current state of the world is
something Rabbi Neil Blumofe says has long been reflected in Jewish
culture. He is the senior rabbi at the Agudas Achim synagogue in
Austin, Texas—one of three synagogues on the campus of the Dell
Jewish Community Center, which also includes a day school, fitness
center, and pool that is open to the entire community, regardless of
one's faith. As you can imagine, security is tight. Blumofe points out
that Jews have never had the luxury of not worrying about security

and refers to the Talmud, a primary source of Jewish religious law and theology, where there is much about identity, community, and the duty to protect. "Throughout our history there has been many times where Jews and synagogues and communities have not felt safe and that has been a very important and very traumatic part of our understanding of the world and how things are now," Blumofe says.[13] Looking to the Psalms, Blumhofe recounts Psalm 137 about how to sing the Lord's song in a foreign land:

> By the rivers of Babylon—
>   there we sat down and there we wept
>   when we remembered Zion.
> On the willows there
>   we hung up our harps.
> For there our captors
>   asked us for songs,
> and our tormentors asked for mirth, saying,
>   "Sing us one of the songs of Zion!"
> How could we sing the LORD's song
> in a foreign land?[14]

For Jews, an ongoing issue is how to preserve themselves and their safety in a world where they are in exile. Blumofe says that while Jewish theology and teachings certainly justify the duty to protect those who enter a synagogue, it's more the long and painful history and experiences of the Jewish people that reflects the unapologetically tight security we find today. "It would be unheard of in this day and age for a synagogue not to have any security plan, and that is both because of things that have happened recently, and because of a shadow of collective memory that goes not only to the Holocaust but back into the Middle Ages with the Crusades, as well as other discriminatory laws that have been passed against Jews in both Europe and Arab majority cultures and, frankly, all over the world."[15]

Realistic yet loving. It's a lot to balance, and yet our traditions call us to do just that for the sake of all those we serve and all those who might be transformed. What this balanced risk and thoughtfulness might look like in the Christian tradition is expressed by

Dr. Catherine Meeks, director of the Absalom Jones Episcopal Center for Racial Healing in Atlanta, Georgia. She often says that the faithful are not called to be comforted in their walk of faith but to be courageous, and one of her signature phrases is her constant request of Christians to be "half a shade braver." One of the oldest images of Jesus in the Christian tradition is that of Jesus as the Good Shepherd. In the tenth chapter of the Gospel of John, Jesus describes himself as the Good Shepherd who loves his sheep so much that he is willing to give his life for them. His care for them is based on what is good for them, not what is good for himself, and he describes the relationship between a true shepherd and his sheep: "My sheep hear my voice. I know them, and they follow me."[16] While I'm certainly not advocating self-sacrifice, the point of a church safety plan is to avoid putting pastors, congregants, and visitors in danger in the first place. It should also avoid putting the onus on one person; we can all be charged with protecting those around us in realistic and faithful ways. In an interview with the national Episcopal Church Women, Meeks offered a prayer that might be useful as we move forward:

> Help us to be brave enough to tell the truth to ourselves and to others.
>
> Help us to be compassionate. Help us to hear the words from You that will fill us with wisdom, peace, and courage.
>
> Help us to be faithful and filled with faith—Amen.[17]

CHAPTER 5

Our Call to Welcome

When you enter a store in Paris and the shopkeeper or sales assistant calls out "Bonjour," it is considered the height of rudeness if you do not respond with a return greeting. If they are not working with other customers, they may come over to ask how they can be of assistance and sometimes they stick pretty close by. If your shopping style and preference is more the American self-serve approach, this welcome can feel as though you are in a spotlight accompanied by the uneasy feeling that you suddenly want to leave, especially if you are just looking with no plans to buy!

The next time you walk into a store or business, notice how you're greeted. Does someone say hello? Do they ask if you need help? Do they even know you're there? These were all questions the US banking industry began to consider in the early 2000s. With bank robberies holding steady at a thirty-year rate of 11 percent per year, banks made a focused effort to start reducing these crimes. Borrowing from a page of Walmart and Home Depot greeting practices (or maybe French shopkeepers), security experts directed bank tellers and employees to greet everyone who walked in the door. This tactic was widely pushed by Seattle FBI agent Larry Carr, who spent five years studying bank robberies and interviewing those who were caught.[1] In his research, he discovered that bank robbers heavily relied on going unnoticed and anything that disrupted that notion was a blow to their confidence and plan. Carr came to believe that a successful case wasn't necessarily apprehending and prosecuting the robber, but instead stopping the robbery from ever happening. In a program called SafeCatch, Carr began training bank workers on the simple premise that by paying attention, you can better control the security of your environment.[2] Carr says the hardest part of implementing SafeCatch was convincing bank managers he wasn't asking employees to do anything aggressive or put their safety at risk. Rather, he wanted them to see how a few preventative measures could easily be implemented and go a long way in increasing security. "You know what, the biggest challenge is overcoming forty years of 'this is the way we've always done it.' The banking industry is a huge ship with a small rudder I have found, not unlike most big organizations. And you know one of the things is it doesn't cost anything. But it is getting over the hurdle."[3] Due to Carr's training and the banks' willingness to try the new form of greeting, Seattle saw a 51 percent decrease in the number of bank robberies in 2008, cutting in half its decade average of approximately three hundred robberies per year.[4]

Banks aren't the only businesses that employ this tactic and chances are good you've been on the receiving end of it. In fact, notice the next time you walk into a service-oriented business like a Super Cuts. The question may seem naïve: "What brings you here today?" The answer is obvious—a haircut. But the question requires an answer and allows the receptionist to engage the customer in conversation.[5] In reflecting on his many trips to Jerusalem where he has had numerous conversations about his trip itinerary and experiences with custom agents and guards, Rabbi Blumoffe said, "It's not just about did you pack your own bag. It's 'Welcome, what are you doing, how did you get here?' and this starts two miles from the airport at the first checkpoint. By the time you get to the gate, you've been seen at least four times."[6] This tactic of asking questions that require a response is what police officers and those in church security now call "upping the greeting game."

During a security walk through in 2019, Austin police officer Joshua Visi told me every church with which he contracts security services, regardless of its faith or size, wrestles with the same dilemma of increasing security while still being welcoming. Some places are asking visitors for more information up front, including names and phone numbers or an email address for follow-up contact. Others are assigning one clergyperson to be present with greeters to assist in welcoming new people. Newcomers are not only asked their names, or if they need help finding the sanctuary, but also if they have any particular prayer needs or want to schedule a welcome call for later in the week to answer questions. If it seems much too simple to work, consider this: after being arrested for the shooting at Mother Emanuel, Roof told FBI agents he was surprised when no one greeted or questioned him when he walked in the church. He went so far to say that if someone had approached him, he might have been too nervous to move forward with his plan.[7] As with the bank robbers who counted on not being noticed, just this small exchange could have thrown Roof enough to ruin his confidence. It also might have helped identify him during earlier visits to the church as someone who warranted a more serious look by church personnel or law enforcement.

Security consultant Bryan Flannery describes his work with faith-based organizations as unique because houses of worship are one of the few places in the business of welcoming the marginalized. "You're certainly protecting your congregation, your flock, so to speak, but you're also protecting the individual who may be on what we call the pathway to targeted violence."[8] Flannery recounts a story about a man who showed up for worship and "all the hairs on the back of the neck of everybody" stood up. The man seemed suspicious, not just to the security team but to many in the congregation, who expressed their concern with his odd behavior of wandering around during worship. The security team discussed it and on the next Sunday when he showed up for church, one of the team members initiated a conversation with him. What they discovered was that this individual was autistic and as the noise level increased during worship (the choir singing, the sermon being delivered, babies crying), the man got more agitated, which led to his walking around and appearing upset. Now knowing this, the church purchased a pair of noise canceling headphones that the man started wearing to make services more comfortable and easier to take part in. "The question I ask is how many times has that guy been pushed down the road at other houses of worship that didn't have this in place?"[9] What we see in this case is a combination of radical hospitality and community-based threat assessment that places of faith around the country are aiming to combine. By pairing these, volunteers and pastoral leaders are finding they can better assist those who might need help or want to be more connected while also providing better security in the process.

Hospitality is one of the fundamental teachings of the Bible. In the stories and teachings of the desert cultures that we find in scripture, the stranger is always welcomed. In Genesis 18, Abraham sees three strangers from the entrance of his tent. He runs out to them, bows low before them, offers them water to wash the burning sands from their feet, a place to rest in the shade, and the finest that he has to eat. They are later identified as angels (hence the reference in Hebrews, "Do not neglect to show hospitality to strangers, for by doing that some have entertained angels without knowing it."), but had they been merchants or shepherds, the faithful response would still have been the same.[10] It is startling to realize that the great sin of Sodom, despite years of moralistic preaching, is not homosexuality; it is the failure of the townspeople in Genesis 19 to treat the strangers in their midst with hospitality.

Contrasting the welcome offered by Abraham (and Lot, in Sodom) with the townspeople of Sodom, Rabbi Stephen S. Pearce suggests that these stories represent a marked contrast "between depravity and disregard for outsiders on one hand, and kindness, generosity, and hospitality to strangers on the other." He later quotes the Talmud on the centrality of radical welcome: "Welcoming guests is greater than welcoming the Divine Presence" (Babylonian Talmud, Shabbat 127a).[11] A truly faithful congregation—and society—extends hospitality to those who need it, whoever and whatever they might be, and these teachings extend well into Christian life. The Benedictines, for example, offered hospitality to all travelers, and the Rule of Benedict asks monastics to greet every person as if she or he is Christ. It also suggests discernment in that welcome that might be illustrative for us:

> All guests who present themselves are to be welcomed as Christ, for he himself will say: I was a stranger and you welcomed me (Matt 25:35). Proper honor must be shown to all, especially to those who share our faith (Gal 6:10) and to pilgrims. Once a guest has been announced, the superior and the brothers are to meet him with all the courtesy of love. First of all, they are to pray together and thus be united in peace, but prayer must always precede the kiss of peace because of the delusions of the devil.[12]

The "kiss of peace" or the sign of peace is offered before a Christian community shares the Eucharist (which represents the complete and total acceptance of a stranger), and it's interesting to note that Benedict advised his monastics to simultaneously offer radical welcome and to observe those who are welcomed before trusting them completely. In church security planning, the second half of Matthew 10:16 is often quoted: "So be wise as serpents and innocent as doves." Perhaps this is Benedict's practical advice about how to combine innocence and wisdom in a church setting.

There is, of course, an implicit risk in welcoming the stranger. The man or woman who walks in off the desert may or may not be a person of good character. Jesus speaks a parable about a burglar in the canonical Gospels (Matthew 12, Mark 3, and Luke 11, respectively) as well as in the Gospel of Thomas. This story suggests that the people of first-century Palestine were well aware that not everyone they encountered deserved their trust, and some could be dangerous. Extending welcome to all can carry some peril. But the danger of not helping someone who is truly in spiritual or material need—and the danger of losing part of one's humanity because of fear—dictate that radical welcome is a risk the faithful must take. Tim Tutt says that, above all, we should not let the fears of the present moment outweigh our central spiritual calls. "The values of love, respect, dignity and peace, grace and caring, assuming the best about people, those are values that maybe are more foundational than the ebb and flow of gun violence."[13] In reflecting on teachings from Thomas Aquinas, Scott Bader-Saye says:

> Avoiding the safe path in order to do the good is what courage calls us to do, that's the nature of courage. But among those key virtues is also the virtue of prudence, which is our capacity to take wise action in the face of particular, contingent events around us. So, to be prudent is also a way of trying to protect the good that has come within our orbit, and that might mean taking certain kinds of safety measures.[14]

Prudence is a way of protecting our churches within a framework of wise faithfulness while courage requires us to assume the best of everyone who comes through the door, even if it's risky. "If you have greeters who are trained outside the synagogue or church or right within the doors to greet and not just say 'welcome' but 'what brings you to church today? What are you looking forward to today?' that kind of thing. . . . I don't see that as a disruption of welcoming," Rabbi Blumofe says. "I see that actually as a very specific and sophisticated way of both welcoming people who should be there and giving a notice to those who shouldn't."[15]

When we look at combining these two values—welcoming and safety—we must strike a balance. "I think the Anglican theology comes to our rescue," says Chuck Treadwell. "One of the core pieces of who we are as Episcopalians is that the truth is in the middle somewhere. . . . When we get off on one of those ideological ends, we fall into sin and dangerous territory. We use our wisdom, we use our reason, we use scripture and tradition and bring all of the resources we have and ask what's smart, what's reasonable, what's holy. I think we can do both."[16]

Given the growing threat to faith communities and the growing need for spiritual connection in an increasingly fragmented society, being safe and welcoming are values that should not be in competition with each other but should mutually reinforce our desire and commitment to each of them. It's a hard balance; we can appreciate the need while lamenting the fact that it is needed. In the *Christian Century*, JoAnn A. Post describes her own experience wrestling to find this balance in changing times:

> Each congregation faces its own unique challenges. Each congregation sets its own goals. Each congregation determines its own threshold beyond which concerns for perceived safety undermine the agility of its ministry. I believe that a church cannot promise complete safety and security. It can only promise to be a trustworthy place, a place where the safety of all is taken seriously, but where the always risky act of welcoming the stranger remains key to its mission.[17]

Across our circumstantial differences and across our faith traditions, we are all called to welcome, even in the face of danger, and our security plan should reflect that as faithfully, lovingly, and safely as possible.

CHAPTER 6

Making a Plan

Whether you've been thinking about it for years or just a few weeks (or you've started and stopped more times than you'd like to admit), it's time to make a security and safety plan for your church. Remember, this is not a plan based on fear and every bad thing that *could* happen; rather, it's a plan that is thoroughly thought out with the intent of creating standards, protocols, and systematic responses to reduce anxiety and increase clarity in emergency situations. This plan will also reflect your house of worship's theology and understanding of where God is in times of trial. The Jewish Reform book of prayer includes the teaching "Pray as if everything depended on God. Act as if everything depended on you." The Bible is full of stories about the essential need for preparation, even for faithful followers of God. The sixth and seventh chapters of Genesis tell the familiar story of Noah's preparation for a world-shaking flood. Although Noah knew he had God's favor, he also acted according to God's wishes: building an enormous ark of cypress, gathering his family and a pair of every animal on earth, and watching for the conditions under which the plans had to be put into practice.

Another biblical figure, Joseph, interpreted the Egyptian pharaoh's dream for God's will and argued for the gathering of food in a time of plenty in preparation for a time of famine. Pharaoh approved:

> Pharaoh said to his servants, "Can we find anyone
> else like this—one in whom is the spirit of God?" So
> Pharaoh said to Joseph, "Since God has shown you
> all this, there is no one so discerning and wise as
> you. You shall be over my house, and all my people
> shall order themselves as you command; only with
> regard to the throne will I be greater than you.[1]

Jesus, too, taught about the interplay of faith and preparation.
I've already mentioned Jesus's teaching about being aware of the
robber who would break into your house and steal from you. In
the parable of the ten bridesmaids, Jesus spoke of ten young women
who were invited to await the coming of the bridegroom:

> Then the kingdom of heaven will be like this. Ten
> bridesmaids took their lamps and went to meet the
> bridegroom. Five of them were foolish, and five
> were wise. When the foolish took their lamps, they
> took no oil with them; but the wise took flasks of
> oil with their lamps.[2]

When the bridegroom arrives in the middle of the night, the
wise women light their lamps and go to greet him. The foolish ones
realize their mistake, ask the wise ones for help, and end up being
completely left out as they try to rectify their error; but it's too late.
Preparation is essential. While this parable is usually taught as a
story about the Last Judgment, Jesus's admonishment of the foolish
ones applies to all of us trying to safeguard our houses of worship:
"Keep awake therefore, for you know neither the day nor the hour."[3]
The biblical record enjoins us to pray and to be prepared for events
we cannot foresee at this moment, but which are all too possible.

In the January 2020 survey of Protestant churches, two out of
three pastors reported that their church had a safety plan. Often
these plans included responses to nonviolent emergencies like fire,
earthquake, tornados, and the need for medical assistance. This
survey also found larger churches were more likely to have a plan for
responding to an active shooting situation.[4] As you dive into this

work, I suggest making your plan as comprehensive as possible given that many different kinds of emergencies can often dovetail with each other. Because everyone reading this will be at a different point in their planning process, I'll start at the beginning.

Creating a Task Force

Gathering a group of people who are interested and committed to this effort is an essential part of this process. Yes, it would be much easier and possibly more efficient to simply assign three or four people to the work, but a task force is better able to provide various perspectives and ultimately create a larger buy-in from a range of stakeholders and groups within your congregation. In Acts, the twelve apostles invite the church to create a task force, "Brothers and sisters, choose seven men from among you who are known to be full of the Spirit and wisdom. We will turn this responsibility over to them and will give our attention to prayer and the ministry of the word."[5]

Seek diversity as you launch this task force, not just agreement. The Gospels and the early church offer us examples: When Jesus gathered his disciples, they weren't a monolithic group. His disciples were fishermen, a tax collector (Matthew), and a revolutionary (Simon). As Martin Luther King Jr. noted, "Jesus recognized the need for blending opposites."[6] Often staff people will be part of your working group, but a number of its members should be parishioners as well. Start identifying a list of candidates who reflect different ages, backgrounds, ethnicities, and life experiences. I'd also consider what populations of your church may feel like they need representation and think about who would do this well. Additionally, identify who has already voiced concerns about safety and might be happy to contribute to this process. I have found the following to be essential people to include:

- The lead pastor or someone who has the ability to speak for that person or act as a liaison to them (such as a parish administrator or operations manager). Regardless of the plan you come up with, your clergy leader is going to have to commit to and support everything it entails.

- The facilities manager, lead sexton, or whatever title you have given to the person who knows every inch of the mechanical operations of your building and could walk you through it blindfolded. This person is crucial when it comes to knowing who to call to fix or replace locks on doors or to test alarms if your plan is going to take into account all emergency scenarios. This would also be a good time to consider including anyone in your parish who has historical knowledge of the architecture of your building, including renovations and expansions. When I have faced questions like, "Why was this door sealed shut?" or "Why doesn't this interior fire wall extend past this point?" it was helpful to locate someone with the answers.

- The director or manager of communications. Speaking as someone who has done communications my entire professional life, hear me when I say a good communications person will help your task force convey plans, progress, and changes to your members in a succinct and clear manner. A good communications person will make sure you are transparent in your process as well as predict the concerns or difficult questions that may arise and help generate responses to them. Smaller congregations who do not have someone in this position should identify a person who is gifted in doing this work.

- Look for people in your congregation who are past or present first responders of any sort (police, fire, EMT). These have been my favorite people to work with and hear their perspectives. There's no substitute for someone telling you the way it's *really* done—especially if they have experience in your own town.

- Identify someone who can bring the mental health and awareness perspective to your conversation and plan. More and more places of worship are requesting mental health awareness training for staffs and worship leadership teams. If anyone in your congregation has experience in the field, invite them to join.

- Consider anyone who has been a victim of gun violence and whether they are willing to be part of this process or an advocate for it—especially if your plan is going to include a pastoral care strategy following a tragic incident. After creating a task force at St. David's, I learned two of our parishioners had witnessed the sniper shooting that took place from the top of the University of Texas tower in 1966. It never occurred to me these were people who could lend perspective to the chaos, confusion, and personal aftermath of such an event.

In working together and formulating your plan, your task force will reflect on both hope and reality, on faith in God and earthly actualities. In King's words, "Jesus reminds us that the good life combines the toughness of the serpent and the tenderness of the dove. To have serpent-like qualities devoid of dovelike qualities is to be passionless, mean, and selfish. To have dovelike without serpent-like qualities is to be sentimental, anemic, and aimless. We must combine strongly marked antitheses."[7] A well-chosen task force can live into the hard tensions of this work as they apply a range of different experiences and knowledge to your plan.

Establish Objectives and Goals

Once your task force team is determined, create a statement of the high-level objective for the group; it can be as simple as, "Due to the increase and concerns of shootings at places of worship, this task force will create a comprehensive plan that addresses security and safety in the building and standard operating procedures for responding to all emergency situations." It's not unusual for task forces to realize that, while mass shooting incidents may have initiated the conversation, safety concerns like fire or medical emergencies have exponentially higher likelihoods of happening and no protocols to handle them exist. Now is an opportunity to formulate a comprehensive plan to address all these things. As you define your objectives, be sure to take into consideration what your goals are for weekdays—when mostly staff and perhaps some outside groups are in the building—versus Saturdays or Sundays when the building is full of worshippers.

The National Cathedral in Washington did exactly this when reassessing its plan. During the week, the church is a popular tourist destination. If something were to happen, whether it be a shooting or a fire, most of the people present wouldn't be familiar with the locations of the nearest exits. This prompted the cathedral's security team to better mark exits, identify escape routes, and put in place protocols for assisting people in the event of an emergency. As your task force sets out objectives, also determine the key areas that might need some extra theological attention. Over the course of this book we've discussed hospitality, the need to protect, and feelings around guns and/or armed officers. Are there clear ideas or a consensus on what constitutes too much, too little, or reasonable actions? This is a good time to reflect on the church's mission, what plans are in place, what is working, what isn't, and where there may need to be some in-depth discussions as the process moves forward. Lastly, I would encourage the task force to make prevention the first and most important goal. While planned responses are absolutely needed, if you can prevent a person or officer from ever pulling out a gun in your sacred space, isn't that the best plan? Before detailing a plan on how to respond to an emergency situation (whatever it may be), ask, "Is there something we can do to prevent or reduce the chances of it even happening?"

Create a Task List

The best way to start your task list is to set an appointment with your local police department for a free risk-assessment walk-through. Generally, this task will be assigned to (or you can request) the district representative for your sector. This is a good way to get to know one of the officers who routinely patrols your area and also knows exactly what kind of criminal activity is taking place in the neighborhood. As I mentioned, prevention is key, so think of your security as a ring of concentric circles; start with securing the outside and move in. As you begin your assessment, take notes and photos for later review. Almost all of the things in your walk-through will be tasks that can be categorized into such groupings as "locks" or "lighting" and organized based on priority and cost. Here are a few things you can expect to discuss during your assessment.

Outside Perimeter

- Security Cameras: Do you have/need them? Are they functioning? Do they need to be repositioned?

- Access Points: How many are there, and can some of them be eliminated? Do doors self-close quickly and properly? Does (or would) a fence help limit entry points into such areas as a playground or garden?

- Lighting: Prior to your risk assessment, walk your campus at night and note if there are any dark areas. Are there areas where motion-detecting lighting would be useful? As bulbs burn out, replace them with LED lights for longer lifespans.

- Implement CPTED (Crime Prevention through Environmental Design): Trees and shrubs immediately surrounding your building should be cut to three feet or lower as to not obstruct windows and help eliminate hiding spots. CPTED includes using plants like cactus and roses bushes to discourage sleeping and loitering around the building. Additionally, remove any hand-sized rocks that could be picked up and thrown, especially around windows and glass doors.

Inside Your Building

- Entrances and Exits: Entry and exit points are generally the low hanging fruit, at least in terms of cost, where significant changes can be made. Most places of worship now have moved to a single point of entry for visitors and worshippers. Not only is this less confusing for those who might not be familiar with your church, it also presents the opportunity we have discussed to be more focused on your welcome strategy. If you have multiple entrances, consider a location such as the front steps or near the parking lot where someone could stand and greet everyone as they arrive before branching off to separate entry points.

- Doors and Locks: St. David's is four stories and spans an entire city block, and I have tested every door and lock in it. While you may not want to spend your visiting officer's time doing this, make time to walk your building on your own for this purpose. Note if any doors no longer shut properly, need a lock installed, or require a crash bar to get out. While working with one church, we discovered doors that were locked for security purposes presented a fire hazard because there was no easy way to exit them. Anytime you plan to permanently lock a door to keep someone out, also ask if you could accidently be locking someone *in*.

- Lighting: Make sure exit signs are visible and well lit, especially during evening hours when lighting tends to be dimmed for services or events.

- High Tech Security Measures: Implementing high tech security measures is where money really becomes a factor, and there's no point in spending a lot of time and resources on something that isn't needed or won't be fully utilized due to a lack of staffing. Also consider its functionality. Upon the implementation of magnetometers (commonly referred to as metal detectors) at Trinity Church Wall Street, the biggest complaint from parishioners was they slowed down entrance into the church on a busy morning and many people found themselves still standing in line as the service began. What the security team quickly realized was that unlike at an airport, where strangers are hoping to get through fast and catch a flight, those in line knew each other and greetings and conversations amongst members slowed the process considerably. As a result, a person was hired to manage the line and have people ready when it was their turn. This resulted in a much more efficient process.[8] At Washington National Cathedral, Jim Shepherd and his security team opted for handheld wands as a way of moving large crowds through security faster. Shepherd noted they can speed things up by only "wanding" every two, three, or five people if the line gets too long. Whatever security needs you have, this is the ideal time to address the options and how the technology would be paid for, implemented, and maintained.

Immediate Internal Communications

How do or would your volunteers, staff, and worship leaders communicate in an emergency situation? Two-way radios are often the cheapest and most effective way to link people who are spread out over a large campus or multiple buildings. Consider whether a mass notification system like Alertus, which allows you to send out campus-wide alerts via speakers, desktops, and cell phones, would be worth the cost. (College campuses are opting for these types of programs, which is how many students and parents are now alerted to on-campus situations.) Or, perhaps, setting up a group chat on an app like GroupMe would be plenty for your weekly staff or

Saturday/Sunday worship leaders. Whatever communication method you decide on, train staff and volunteers on how to use it. In any emergency situation, immediate and reliable communication will be imperative for a quick response.

Increase Awareness and Reporting Procedures

Just days after the 2019 shooting at a Walmart in El Paso, Texas, Melissa Potter got an unexpected call from her nephew. It was odd because she didn't really have a relationship with him, but she thought something might be wrong, so she answered. On the other end Brandon Wagshol asked if he could use her New Hampshire address to ship high-capacity magazines to her home because he couldn't get them sent to his house in Connecticut, where magazines with that many rounds were banned. He also told her about his plans to build an AR-15 style rifle. Knowing Wagshol's troubled past, Potter reached out to local authorities and the case eventually found its way to the FBI. Based on prior documented threats of mass violence, authorities were able to search Wagshol's residence, where they found hundreds of rounds of ammunition, several guns, a grenade, and body armor. Wagshol was arrested and a tragedy was most likely averted.[9]

Like Wagshol's aunt, we rarely see the full picture of an incident unfolding. She knew that the phone call was concerning and that his past was problematic, but she had no way of knowing what was hidden in his house or about any plans he may have had to actually carry out a violent act. Yet she was concerned enough to say something, despite possibly being wrong and upsetting her extended family. Raising awareness among your worship community and discussing how to report a concern is one of—if not *the*—most valuable area to spend your time and effort. Create and communicate a reporting policy so that staff members and congregants feel safe and know how to inform a church administrator or leader if there is a concern or a domestic situation that could unfold at church. Considering you can do this at almost no cost by preparing your own security guide that includes protocols for reporting and how emergencies will be handled, the return on your investment is huge.

Active Shooter Training and Drills

When panicked, people in your congregation will look toward those in an official capacity to measure their own responses and determine how to react. Training offers those in your church an opportunity to learn and, just as importantly, provide a forum to ask questions. The more people feel that they are part of the process, the better off you will be as you work to increase awareness and create a culture of safety. In an article for the *Washington Post* following the Tree of Life shooting, Mark Berman wrote about how active-shooter trainings can save lives:

> When a gunman opened fire inside Pittsburgh's Tree of Life synagogue last fall, Stephen Weiss heard gunshots and saw shell casings hit the floor. He was about to get down when he remembered the active shooter training that taught him to flee. "I didn't have time to stand there and question myself . . . I just had to do something," said Weiss, a schoolteacher. The training kicked in, Weiss recalled in an interview, and he fled. "That ten seconds was probably the difference between me living or not."[10]

One of the best, most cost-effective approaches to training sessions is to reach out to your local law enforcement agency and see what they offer. Many agencies are training officers in the Civilian Response to Active Shooter Events (CRASE) course, which was designed and built on the Avoid, Deny, Defend strategy developed by ALERRT at Texas State University. I've hosted and attended half a dozen of these trainings, and what I like about this program's approach is the initial focus on raising awareness, followed by what can be done to increase the chances of survival should someone be involved in such an event. Learning, for example, how dozens of lives were spared during the Virginia Tech shooting because students were able to lock or barricade classroom doors and deny entry is critical. When the shooter couldn't gain entry, he then returned to other unlocked classrooms he had already attacked and began shooting again. The locked doors made all the difference. Tabletop exercises can also be effective ways for people to discuss how they would react given a certain scenario and location.

I want to address mock drills since the question comes up often. In general, I'm not a fan of them. I say "in general" because I think it is one thing to do a tightly controlled mock drill with a trained security team, each of whom is prepared for the mental, physical, and emotional elements of that kind of situation, versus exposing ordinary people to that kind of stress and anxiety. If you decide to have a drill, do not—under any circumstances—present it as a surprise or real event. I don't have to go into the emotional trauma or the physical risks this could cause if people think an actual gunman is in the building. If you want to train people to exit the quickly, hold a planned and announced fire drill. You'd be surprised what problems and obstacles are exposed on such a basic level.

I would be remiss not to draw attention to some of the many conferences and gatherings churches do to consolidate efforts and offer training on a wider scale. The cathedral of the Rockies Methodist Church in Boise, Idaho, put on its first Safe Church Summit in 2016. The following year, it offered a two-day conference in which attendees explored everything from active shooter training to safe child protocols and cyber security. In the Episcopal Diocese of New Hampshire, several churches hosted trainings led by Blue-U Defense, a group of off-duty and retired law enforcement officers. These trainings were open to all faith communities in the area. Following one such training, New Hampshire Bishop Rob Hirschfeld told the Episcopal News Service, "I'm encouraged by people coming away from this with a sense of reasonableness; they're less panicked, more empowered, more aware of the space they're in and the possibilities to frustrate the intent of those who wish to do harm. And that's good."[11] The Consortium of Endowed Episcopal Parishes (CEEP) offers at least one session on safety and security each year at its annual conference, providing a great forum to share information and resources. Be on the lookout for opportunities and resources available in your community and within your faith tradition as you move forward in your planning.

Mental Health Education and Disruption Policies

As I mentioned earlier, more and more congregations are requesting mental health education as they aim to reduce the stigma related to mental illness and better learn how to handle disruptions or incidents that result from mental illness. Most police departments have officers who are specially trained in mental health responses and can be dispatched to help. Teaching verbal de-escalating tactics to staff, ushers, and greeters is an important security measure to ensure everyone's safety until help arrives. This doesn't mean you have to completely defuse a situation; in fact, I often think of de-escalation as a stall tactic that prevents a situation from getting worse (assuming it's manageable in the moment). The National Alliance on Mental Illness (NAMI) is a good place to start if you're looking for resources or training. The Austin chapter of NAMI offers a training workshop for houses of worship presented in conjunction with the local police department. The hour-and-a-half session aims to address mental health myths and lay out what to expect if you call 911 for help. This is also a good time to review or update your disruption policy. This certainly doesn't mean all disruptions are created by someone with mental health issues, but often that is the case.

A disruption policy is important for several reasons. First, it immediately puts into action a plan to address the situation; no wasting time figuring out who is going to do what. Second, a disruption policy ensures everyone else that any incident will be safely handled as quickly as possible and allows them to focus on why they are there—to worship. As we know, feeling safe is more important to congregants than ever, and offering a sense of safety is an essential part of welcoming people into our spaces. In creating or reviewing your policy, be specific as to who will approach the person and how. Depending on the disruption, an usher may be fully capable of politely removing the person from the area. I've seen everything from "Let's go get a cup of coffee," to "Want to join me outside for a cigarette?" used to get the person away from a crowd or out of the building. Many places prefer to handle disruptions as "light-handed" as possible, only calling on hired security or the police if things are more serious or seem to be escalating. A disruption policy should also identify what happens once the person is no longer an immediate concern. Remember, this is one of those crossroads where security and radical hospitality can intersect in a way we are called to serve on both fronts.

Other Emergency Planning

As I mentioned earlier, this is an ideal time to assess all other emergencies and how to best handle them. As with your local police department, you can contact your church insurance company to do a free risk assessment. Keep in mind the insurance company representative will focus on things that could be a liability, such as bookshelves that aren't bolted to the wall or steep steps that aren't properly marked. However, this is a good opportunity to look at where the safest places are in the event of a tornado or if you have an adequate supply of defibrillators and fully stocked first aid kits. Likewise, your local fire department can help you plan a church-wide fire drill and afterward can pinpoint problem areas or issues you need to address. In doing a drill with one church, we discovered that the fire alarm in one particular room was barely audible and the unit needed replacing. We never would have known without the drill. The drill also allowed us to train volunteers on how to "sweep" the building to make sure everyone was out and led to further discussions on how to safely evacuate elderly or disabled members if the elevators shut down. In putting together a safety plan, consider how you would include and address the following emergency situations.

- Fire: Who will help those who are mentally or physically impaired? Where is the designated meeting point once everyone is out of the building?

- Medical Emergency: Who will call for help? Is there adequate medical supplies to treat a person until aid arrives?

- Lockout: How will you notify and lock people down inside the building if there is a threat outside; for example, in the case of civil unrest like what we saw at the Capitol or an escaped inmate or dangerous person in the area.

As you get started, check out the Federal Emergency Management Agency's (FEMA) Faith-Based Community Preparedness page on its website for resources. Even though your staff and members may feel like they know most of the safety procedures, being able to write them down and define them as part of you plan provides clarity so everyone is on the same page.

Communicating Your Plan

All of your preparation will be futile if you don't adequately communicate what you are doing and why. Effective communication about the plan is more than telling your congregants what changes to expect; it includes everything from training manuals for your incoming ushers to signage around the church. It is also important to convey how the plan grows out of and reinforces your mission. Here's an example of what Chuck Treadwell sent out on February 22, 2018, following the Stoneman Douglas High School shooting:

> Last week, I shared in your grief, as I learned of yet another mass shooting in our country. I found myself wrestling with feelings and opinions that came in many forms: that of a husband, of a father, and of a rector of a large downtown parish. I can't

say that I came up with any answers to the deeply disturbing events and divisive debates going on, but I do want to share with you what is being done at St. David's to improve our safety and support our community.

Last month, our director of communications, Jeanie Garrett, created a safety planning task force comprised of staff members and parishioners. This group was thoughtfully created to include staffers in key positions related to safety and parishioners with experience in safety management. With the help of resources from Church Mutual (our insurance provider), FEMA, and the Austin Police Department, this task force is in the process of creating a comprehensive intruder / active shooter plan which includes how to spot warning signs, what to do in the event of a shooting, and specific recommendations for improving our communications during the week and on Sundays. Once this plan is ready, we will have a training session for our staff and vestry members, as well as Sunday support leaders, such as ushers and greeters. I know we can't precisely predict how an event might happen, but through increased awareness and improved communication strategies, we can be better prepared.

I have seen many variations of this message as places of worship begin their security planning. As with Treadwell's email, a personal message from your lead pastor explaining what is being done and why is a good way to start the discussion. It lets people know this effort is being supported at the highest level and is being thoughtfully, and prayerfully, carried out.

As the task force moves ahead, plan to provide weekly or monthly updates to your progress. This is especially important if people will be seeing or experiencing something different when they come on campus, such as a security guard or a reduction in usable entrances.

You'll want to communicate these changes well before they happen in as much detail as possible. Often the backlash over the change isn't necessarily about what is being implemented; it's the feeling of not being heard, or the sense of loss people feel when our sacred spaces are no longer assumed to be completely safe. It helps to designate one or two people to respond to questions, as this mainstreams the process and gives you a clear idea if one question or concern comes up repeatedly. Another effective way to convey your security and safety policies is through manuals for your staff, front desk receptionist, and ushers and greeters. (Often similar content can be used in each of these, with specific policies noted that pertain to each of those positions.) Start with your already existing manuals or policies, then build out from there. Add in any new policies and include some standard information such as basic first aid, de-escalation tactics, and what to do if you see a suspicious package or receive a bomb threat. A quick search on the web will net you free resources and handouts to include in your collateral.

Remember, putting together a security plan doesn't have to be hard or expensive. Often it's just about addressing a need or problem, finding a solution, and communicating that solution so everyone knows what to do. Here's a great example. I worked with a woman who is the receptionist of an urban church that provides free breakfast several times a week for those experiencing homelessness. One of the ongoing problems she had was one of the regular attendees would come into the lobby after breakfast and sit for hours on end. Sometimes they would disappear into a nearby chapel, making it hard to remember they were still on campus. During our security assessment process, we included a written policy that visitors were limited to one hour in the lobby. The policy was placed in a front desk manual that she could point to if needed. It wasn't hard and it cost nothing, but the relief it provided her was immeasurable, and it greatly increased her safety because she was now better aware of who was in the building.

Once you've defined and outlined your policies and plans, you can focus on visually communicating them throughout the church. Consider areas where you might want to better identify where the nearest fire extinguisher, first aid kit, or defibrillator is located. I've seen great examples of room-by-room safety plans that are posted near the door—some are elaborate flip charts while others are just a sectioned sheet of paper that notes the nearest exit, the church's address if you need to call 911, and how to shelter in place in that particular room. These easy-to-read signs should be made with visitors who may be less familiar with your building in mind.

Finally, don't be afraid to admit if something isn't working. Putting it into action might be the only way you'll see the problem and embrace a new, better way to approach it. In Voltaire's words: Don't let the perfect be the enemy of the good. Keep moving forward with your plan, knowing it can be changed and adjusted as you live into its reality and revisit it in the months and years to come.

CHAPTER 7

Common Planning Pitfalls

There's no question that putting together a plan can be daunting. Small changes become bigger issues than you could have possibly foreseen, and costs can add up more quickly than the dollars to cover them. In my experience, the pitfalls to security planning generally fall into three categories: emotional responses, financial costs, and lack of leadership. Knowing how these issues can delay or derail the process can better prepare you for identifying the issues early on and working through them effectively. It's essential to keep pressing on even if there are tasks that have to be tabled for a later date until concerns can be addressed or money allocated.

Pitfall One: Emotional Responses to Change

In *Choosing Hope,* Sandy Hook Elementary teacher Kaitlin Roig-DeBellis writes about the shooting and returning to school after the tragedy. She recalls that her classroom was the first one in the building, and she knew it would be the first one Adam Lanza came to as he shot his way through the school on December 14, 2012. Unlike many of the other classrooms, hers had a tiny bathroom in which she managed to lock fifteen students and herself while Lanza blasted bullets just feet away. If it had not been for a place to hide, she and her students almost certainly would have been among the

75

dead. Upon returning to a new, temporary school one month later, Roig-DeBellis immediately noticed that her new classroom had no such hiding place. Despite the new high-tech security measures, she felt like her still distraught first graders needed to actually see they had a way out if a shooting were to happen again. She lobbied, at the very least, for the school to provide an escape ladder so that she and the students could climb out a window and run. "The principal listened politely until I had finished making my case. 'I don't think it's necessary,' she said. . . . I sensed, at that moment, that our conversation was over and the subject was closed."[1] It's hard to imagine a simple request like this being denied. Unfortunately, this is the exact sort of thing that becomes an issue when emotions of all kinds play into such a sensitive topic.

I can see, on one hand, how the principal may have felt that the school had put dozens of new measures in place, and teachers going rogue with their own security planning might not be the best direction. However, I can more strongly and compassionately understand that this ladder symbolized an emotional safety net for this particular class, and what is the harm in having a tangible sign that the school and teacher are committed to everyone's mental and physical well-being? (Not to mention it being useful in a fire emergency as well!) Downplaying the seriousness of emotional responses to situations and changes or dismissing vulnerabilities that come with these conversations is one of the worst things you can do in your planning. Anxiety will show itself in many ways, including anger, fear, or the collective "but we've always done it this way." (I can't tell you how many times the effort to lock or just close a door was met with a firm: "But that door has always been open.") You don't have to dig very deep into those statements to see that the true loss one is experiencing is that the comfort and ease we have grown to expect is now being replaced with concern and worry. The closed door now signifies the danger that could threaten our church and loved ones and our attempt—possibly futile—to stop it. So, here we are, arguing about a door when the deeper truth of loss is what we are all actually wrestling with inside. Don't shy away from the conversations in which these are discussed. Remember when Joseph Moore realized he just needed to listen to all of the reasons the congregant was afraid? Listening to the concerns and talking through what this change looks and feels like are important steps. It's also important to consider these questions:

- How do we balance the need for safety while respecting long and perhaps important ways of doing things?

- How do we slowly but firmly move the pendulum from old and comfortable to new ways that reflect our modern world?

- How can we see that God is working in our midst?

In answering these questions, Isaiah 43 offers comfort amid challenge. Scholars identify the writing during the time of the Babylonian Exile. For these displaced Hebrews, the old world was gone, and the future was menacing. But God promised to be present even in the new reality:

> But now thus says the LORD,
>   he who created you, O Jacob,
>   he who formed you, O Israel:
> Do not fear, for I have redeemed you;
>   I have called you by name, you are mine.
> When you pass through the waters, I will be with you;
>   and through the rivers, they shall not overwhelm you;
> when you walk through fire you shall not be burned,
>   and the flame shall not consume you.[2]

These promises that God will accompany us through the fire and through the waters are essential in the work we are doing, but the chapter also offers something even more comforting than the reminder of God's presence. In verses 18 and 19, God tells us straight out that God is about to do a new thing, and of course the history of our salvation is that God is always doing something new:

> Do not remember the former things,
>   or consider the things of old.

I am about to do a new thing;
   now it springs forth, do you not perceive it?
I will make a way in the wilderness
   and rivers in the desert.[3]

Remember Catherine Meeks's call to be "a half-shade braver"? Living into change and recognizing it as a part of our call as people of faith means moving from fear of change to faithful embrace. Not that it is easy—as any minister who has changed a worship service knows—but it is an essential part of the growth and vitality of any system, including faith systems. In her novel *Ceremony*, Native American author Leslie Marmon Silko writes of her traditional healer who says that "things which don't shift and grow are dead things. They are things the witchery people want. Witchery works to scare people, to make them fear growth."[4] Martin Luther King Jr. told the story of a segregationist in the South who realized desegregation was inevitable. The man then talked about how he hoped those changes wouldn't take place until after he died, and King responded, "The soft minded man always fears change. He feels security in the status quo, and he has an almost morbid fear of the new. For him, the greatest pain is the pain of a new idea. . . . The soft minded person always wants to freeze the moment and hold life in the gripping yoke of sameness."[5] Ideally, we shouldn't characterize those in our communities who resist change as soft-minded, and we can certainly understand fear and nostalgia for a remembered past. But the point here is clear; things change, wishing they didn't doesn't change that fact, and embracing new ways of thinking, seeing, and doing might actually lead us in the direction of greater faithfulness and joy.

Pitfall Two: Money

As I write this, I'm sitting in our daughters' playroom that is (finally) being converted to my home office. It has been a slow process. I've had to clear out a bookshelf of beloved childhood favorites, clean slime off the ceiling, and box up more American Girl dolls and accessories than anyone should own. Twenty little paint swatches are taped to the wall, and I'm still not sure if I like any of my options. Once the painting is complete, I need to get the carpet professionally cleaned and buy furniture. Much like my office project, safety planning can feel like a very long and slow process and a juggling act of prioritizing your needs with your funds.

It would be easy for many communities of faith to simply say, "We have no money for security planning because we can't even afford the basics." But by this point I hope you have come to see, both theologically and practically, that your congregation can move forward on some level regardless of the obstacles. Recall Jesus's call to his disciples to go out into the countryside and do God's work with little: "Take no gold, or silver, or copper in your belts, no bag for your journey, or two tunics, or sandals, or a staff."[6] Set forth in the direction of your goal. You might be surprised to find that someone in your community will feel led to contribute to this effort or funds can be reallocated to cover some of the expenses. In any case, when we hear that God is doing a new thing, the last thing we want to do is let money be the thing that stands in the way of it, especially when we can go far in the beginning with very little. Start small and cross the easy things off your list. As you review your walk-through notes, decide what can be done for little or no cost (like limiting access points and replacing light bulbs) and what things you'll need to budget for before proceeding. Also, consider where you will get the biggest bang for your buck. If security cameras will greatly increase your security and fulfill several high priority needs, it may be worth purchasing those and letting some of the less expensive things wait. The most important thing to do is to prioritize your needs and set a realistic time and financial plan for the work.

When it comes to church security spending, costs run the spectrum. In a 2019 podcast on church security, Stonegate Fellowship in Midland, Texas, reported spending about $50,000 a year on security while the East Plano Islamic Center in Plano, Texas, spends as much as $150,000 annually.[7] Christ Church Cathedral in Houston found themselves right in the middle, spending about $97,000 for security in 2019.[8] Rob Sokol declined to say how much Trinity Church Wall Street spends, but given the volume and location of its properties, we can assume it's a significant amount. And while Trinity Church has substantially more financial resources than most houses of worship, Sokol warns, "The issue with security cost, in my opinion, is that there's never enough. It is a bottomless pit, financially. There's never enough security to be truly secured."[9] Again, this is why Sokol firmly believes in starting small and with the basics, only increasing such things as the number of officers or technology if need dictates it.

Many mosques, synagogues, and churches are finding ways to build and improve their security with the help of grants. In 2020, a US government program run by FEMA and the Department of Homeland Security increased its grant funding to ninety million dollars, money specifically allocated for faith-based groups to harden security on their buildings. The Secure Community Network provides resources and trainings to synagogues and temples. Although not guaranteed, and often requiring a good amount of work and persistence, grants are a valuable resource, especially if your house of worship might be a significant target due to its nature or location. While a limited budget and a lack of money are often blamed for a lack of security planning, just remember that simple and inexpensive measures, such as creating a culture of awareness, can begin immediately and have far-reaching impacts that can't be measured in dollars.

Pitfall Three: Lack of Leadership and Burnout

Strong leadership and support from the top are vital when taking on safety and security planning. Not only are you making decisions and changing practices that potentially affect every person who walks into your building, but the financial decisions and costs associated with some of these changes will have to be championed and approved if they are going to happen. Who are your decision makers? Is it the head pastor or priest, who makes decisions based on theology and church beliefs? Perhaps the business manager, who holds the purse strings? Or maybe the building supervisor, who has to approve and implement many of the changes? Chances are it's a little bit of all of these people. Identify your key leaders early on and discuss their role and significance in this process. Identifying who needs to check off on what will save you time, energy, and probably a good amount of frustration as your process unfolds. The model of the Good Shepherd speaks back into the lives of church leaders and their importance: they are responsible for the spiritual and physical well-being of those in their communities. Being a good leader also means keeping those involved motivated and focused on the work. Most task forces start with the best intentions, but as the work increases and the issues become more complex, members and volunteers can start to lose steam and, in some cases, burnout completely leaving the plan half-baked and incomplete. For this reason, only recruit volunteers who seem genuinely interested in the project or a certain aspect of it. If you have to spend hours or send repeated emails to get someone on board, it's probably not going to be to the benefit of the team down the road. This is where targeting volunteers with certain skills or perspectives as we discussed earlier is valuable. While you will need key people on the task force for consistency, volunteers with specific interests can be invited to attend sub–task force meetings where that particular topic will be discussed. Regardless of how you plan to hold meetings, set them regularly. In working with First United Methodist Church, we met biweekly on Tuesdays—same time, same place, and always with a clear agenda—which helped us stay on track as we moved through our tasks and deadlines.

Depending on the size of your church and how much you plan to accomplish, I like to keep the entire safety planning process at three to six months, starting with the time a task force is formed and risk assessments begin. Following the assessments, determine deadlines for the physical work that needs to be done as well as the communication pieces and trainings. Trainings should be held toward the end of the process, as this gives you time to see how new procedures are working, become comfortable with the changes, and anticipate questions. It might be helpful to consider all of this work as phase one. Phase two can be designated for six to twelve months later when funds are available for some of the bigger projects and policies might need revisiting. Phase three should be an annual review of the policies and updated training for everyone. While safety and security is an ongoing practice that we must continuously be mindful of, the initial work should be done with the long-term goal of putting a plan into place that will sustain for decades to come.

Reflecting on the three questions of balancing change, being called to something new, and seeing God in our work, we must remember that God is working through us even, or perhaps especially, in the midst of division, chaos, and violence. We choose to be part of it by facing our fears and feelings of loss or anxiety head on and by acknowledging that we are called to be a part of this new thing in both prayer and action.

CHAPTER 8

Social Justice and Cultural Change

It's not enough to make our houses of worship more secure and declare the work is done. If we are to make changes in our churches and sacred spaces because of the violence and chaos outside, doesn't it also make sense to work to change the violence and chaos? For some, "thoughts and prayers" are the limit of what faith communities can offer in response to mass shootings and other violent outrages, but it is clear that thoughts and prayers are not nearly enough. We can and should do more. In a June 6, 2019, Facebook post, CNN's Chris Cuomo called out the moral inertia of thoughts and prayers language:

> Friday there was another mass shooting murder.... What can I say? You know everything. And what you don't know . . . does it matter? The people who made it and how it happened. The panicked recollections of people forever changed by one senseless event. The families whose loved ones are hurt or gone. The urgent interruptions as the latest nugget of detail about what happened or something about the shooter. The type and number and source of the guns. We will be super careful about what we call them because somehow it has become really important not to confuse a regular semiautomatic

with a military style rifle versus an assault rifle or
a machine gun. We put more energy into parlance
than prevention. . . . And you will confuse this one
with others. Only in America . . . let me say it again.
. . . Only in America. . . . Thoughts and prayers. I
see those as an empty gesture but they don't have
to be. Prayer is not a bad thing. It just shouldn't be
the only thing . . .

Like Cuomo and most Americans, I'm sick and tired of these
shootings. I'm sick and tired of hoping more won't happen. Recently,
I was explaining to a new acquaintance how I got involved in church
security work, and why I feel called to do it. For many, the shooting at
Sandy Hook Elementary was a turning point in their thinking about
public violence; I was no exception. At the time of the shooting,
my oldest daughter was in kindergarten, so *this* particular horror—
this particular shooting—hit closer to home than all the others. It
was too easy to imagine. It was eleven days before Christmas, and I
already had presents from Santa wrapped and hidden in my closet.
The idea that the Sandy Hook parents who lost children also had
presents ready and would now face every Christmas without their
child tormented me as I lay in bed at night. I wondered if I was crazy
for letting my own daughter go back to school. The Monday following the shooting, I walked her to her classroom, said goodbye,
and prayed I'd see her that afternoon. Thoughts and prayers . . .

Four months later on April 17, 2013, a visibly upset President
Obama gave a speech in the White House Rose Garden after pro-
posed gun reform legislation failed in the Senate. He was introduced
by Sandy Hook parent Mark Braden, father of Daniel Braden, who
died in his first-grade classroom. "When Newtown happened,"
President Obama said, "I met with these families, and I spoke to
the community and I said, 'Something must be different right now,
we're going to have to change.' That's what the whole country said.
Everybody talked about how we were going to change something
to make sure this didn't happen. Again." The president was furious
and heartbroken, just as many of us were that day when the Senate

didn't pass legislation expanding background checks. He called it "a pretty shameful day for Washington."[1] That's when I came to the realization that it would be up to us—individually and as communities—to help ensure security in the places we expect it most, including our churches. For me, that's when thoughts and prayers turned to action.

At the same time, a newly formed group called Bishops United Against Gun Violence was gaining steam. Connecticut bishop Ian Douglas is one of about one hundred Episcopal Church bishops who make up the network. Douglas says he never expected this issue to be part of his work, but all that changed as he rushed to Newtown on December 14, 2012. St. John's Episcopal Church, which has since closed, was located just up the hill from Sandy Hook Elementary. Due to its proximity, it became an immediate place for the community to gather and grieve following the news of the shooting. Additionally, the family of six-year-old Ben Wheeler, who died in the massacre, attended nearby Trinity Episcopal Church, where national and local media would set up days later when the Wheelers buried their son. In the years since then, Douglas and his counterparts at Bishops United Against Gun Violence have led efforts for change, including meeting with legislators on Capitol Hill and calling for safety measures and reform. "It's not a question of advocacy as much as it is a question of cultural change," Douglas explains. "Not unlike the movement that brought about seat belts and safer cars and anti-smoking cultural change in the United States. That's what we're talking about. Change, awareness, and safety."[2] Douglas doesn't like to think of his work as a social justice ministry because he doesn't believe there is a distinction between the work and the church; the work is the church, he says. He is also mindful that the Episcopal Church is not exempt from being complicit in the manufacturing of guns and in gun violence, particularly in his home state of Connecticut, which has historically been one of the largest producers of firearms in the world. In an article for the *Huffington Post*, Douglas wrote, "It was in Connecticut where the first 'automatic weapons' of the nineteenth century were manufactured. The revolver was invented by Samuel Colt in Hartford in 1836 and the repeating rifle by Horace Smith and Daniel B. Wesson in Norwich in the early 1850s. One of our Episcopal churches, a Colt family legacy, even has revolvers and rifles carved into the brownstone arches adorning the entryways."[3] Douglas thinks it's important to acknowledge this history, but he refuses to let it define the future. The church can (and should) repent of its past actions in order to act more justly going forward.

As we saw in the teaching from Reform Judaism, we are asked to pray diligently about problems—then get to work on them. In the Jewish tradition, the term *tikkun olam* is a central theme that is synonymous with Christian appeals for social justice. Its translation is "repairing the world," and the concept is taught by rabbis to everyone, including young children, since no one is too young or too old, too wise or too broken, to help improve the world and what God has created. On the one-year anniversary of the Tree of Life shooting, community-wide service projects were organized with *tikkun olam* in mind. Acts of *tikkun olam* can also be attempts to right the wrongs of the world, as explained by Rabbi Tzvi Freema,

> Each act of *tikkun olam* is a fine-tuning of our world's voices. With each *tikkun*, we are creating meaning out of confusion, harmony from noise, revealing the unique part each creation plays in a universal symphony that sings of its Creator. This is a deeper meaning of the term *tikkun olam*: The word *olam* also means "hidden." We need to repair the world so that its Creator is no longer hidden within, but shines through each thing in magnificent, harmonious beauty.[4]

The idea of *tikkun olam* lives in many of us, as seen in the 2018 March for Our Lives rally. More than a million demonstrators across the globe marched to bring awareness and call for action to end gun violence. The student-initiated rally came on the heels of the February 14, 2018, Marjory Stoneman Douglas High School shooting in Parkland, Florida, and included survivors like Cameron Kasky. Taking the stage in Washington, DC, the seventeen-year-old high school junior delivered a dynamic and emotional address before an estimated two hundred thousand onlookers:

> We hereby promise to fix the broken system we have been forced into and create a better world for the generations to come. Don't worry, we've got this. . . . We must stand beside those we lost and fix the world that betrayed them. This doesn't just happen in schools. Americans are being attacked in churches, night clubs, movie theaters, and on the streets, but we the people can fix this. For the first time in a long while, I look forward ten years and I feel hope. I see light. I see a system I'll be proud of, but it all starts with you. The march is not the climax of this movement, it is the beginning. It is the springboard off which my generation and all who stand with us will jump into a safer future.

The four-minute speech was powerful and, to Kasky's great credit, could have been summed up in his very first sentence: "To the leaders, skeptics and cynics who told us to sit down and stay silent [and] wait your turn: Welcome to the revolution."[5]

Fifty years earlier, almost to the day, Martin Luther King Jr. stood in the Canterbury pulpit of Washington National Cathedral and spoke of such a revolution in the last Sunday sermon he delivered before his death in Memphis. King drew on the story of Rip Van Winkle from American author Washington Irving for inspiration:

> When Rip Van Winkle went up into the mountain, the sign had a picture of King George the Third of England. When he came down twenty years later the sign had a picture of George Washington, the first president of the United States. When Rip Van Winkle looked up at the picture of George Washington—and looking at the picture he was amazed—he was completely lost. He knew not who he was. And this reveals to us that the most

striking thing about the story of Rip Van Winkle is not merely that Rip slept twenty years, but that he slept through a revolution. While he was peacefully snoring up in the mountain, a revolution was taking place that at points would change the course of history—and Rip knew nothing about it. He was asleep. Yes, he slept through a revolution. And one of the great liabilities of life is that all too many people find themselves living amid a great period of social change, and yet they fail to develop the new attitudes, the new mental responses, that the new situation demands. They end up sleeping through a revolution.[6]

In musing on King's final sermon, *Atlantic Monthly* writer Vann Newkirk says, "King used that example sort of as a parable to warn people about how to remain awake during a great revolution. What he talked about was how to stay woke, as lots of people say. But also how to, if you were in the process of waking up, how to have your racial awakening, and how to get to the point where you could critically engage with life, with race, with becoming an anti-racist."[7]

This notion rings true of many other social justice initiatives where people are called to work together so that our world might better reflect God's kingdom. Kelly Brown Douglas writes about our "moral participation" in the world and, quoting Peruvian theologian Gustavo Gutierrez, describes it as "having an active presence in history."[8] She goes on to describe moral participation as the things we do and believe that actively reflect Jesus in our world and God's kingdom as it could be, not as it presently is. This requires "moral imagination," which is what King inspires us to do in thinking past where we are and instead look to where we could be, even if that vision seems far out of reach in the moment. "A moral imagination is grounded in the absolute belief that the world can be better," Douglas writes. "What is certain, a moral imagination disrupts the notion that the world as it is reflects God's intentions."[9] Waking up to God's intentions as revealed in scripture, tradition, and individual revelation becomes a central goal for all of us who seek to make the world better.

Following Saturday's March for Our Lives rally, the Rev. Phil Jackson stood before a Sunday crowd at Trinity Church Wall Street and delivered an impassioned sermon about gun violence drawn from the Gospel of Mark's passage on Jesus being brought in front of Pilate. Pilate offered the gathered crowd a choice between the itinerant wonder worker Jesus and the revolutionary Barabbas, a choice that would define who they were and demonstrate their moral imagination, or lack of it.

> This is the choice the people had, Barabbas or Jesus. One's a nationalist, one says love your enemies. Barabbas is a man of violence who believes that any form of resistance and fighting against the Roman overlords was acceptable. Jesus said, "Blessed are the peacemakers." Barabbas said that "evils are all external to us. Drive out the Romans and all will be well." Jesus called for repentance and a turning back to God.[10]

Jackson's eloquence and passion shone as he singled out the moral choices of privileging guns over our children.

> And now we are willing to say, "Well, that happens." And that's unacceptable. It's unacceptable. We're willing to turn our backs when children say, "I don't want to get killed in school. I don't want to see my friends get killed in school." And we adults act as if what? "Oh, well, you know, that's the price we're willing to pay." And that, my friends, is insane. That's insane. Because children . . . children shouldn't have to worry about that, not at school, not at home, not in the street, not anywhere. Children shouldn't have to worry about getting killed. Why? Because we feel that the higher value is to own a gun. The higher value is the future. And

the future [is] children. . . . What does it say about us, what does it say about us that we will put the future off and tell the future "We don't really care about you; we like you but we don't really care about you, because to own this gun is more important than you?" You know that's what we're saying, right? And we say it over, and over, and over again. . . . Who are you going to choose? Now, let me just map this out. There's no stretch of the imagination that I can make by which I would say that in the realm of the Kingdom of God that in what it means to be a Christian that owning a gun is more important than a child's life. I can't possibly say that. I can't possibly make that claim. And I don't believe we can either, can we? Who're you going to choose, Barabbas or Jesus?[11]

As with the young Cameron Kasky, merely reading these words on paper doesn't come close to conveying the moral participation and imagination both men speak about and deliver so fervently. Moral participation requires us to keep our values at the forefront; to keep talking about them, to keep fighting for them, and to keep imagining how those values might manifest in the kingdom of God.

The Rev. Deanna Hollas is doing just this in a newly created position in the Presbyterian Church (USA). In July 2019, Hollas was named the first minister of gun violence prevention and given a full-time mission as coordinator of gun violence prevention ministries of the Presbyterian Peace Fellowship. She describes her role as one that encourages the Presbyterian Church to become informed and engaged in ending gun violence. Initially, this meant providing resources to congregations, but her calling then expanded to coordinating voting information for the 2020 general election and supporting the more controversial effort to defund local police programs. "Right now what we're saying is that as a society where we are pouring all of our money is into a system of domination, a system of harm, and a system of punishment," Hollas said. "What we know is that doesn't lead to any type of change."[12] Hollas would rather see the cost of guns and ammunition increase and be taxed at a level that makes them harder to afford. She also suggests using the sales of guns and ammunition to fund police in a reciprocal relationship of gun violence to the need for law enforcement. It's not a far-fetched idea seeing how external sources of funding could be needed as city councils across the country have drastically cut police budgets, including those in large metropolitan areas like Los Angeles, which faced a $150 million cut to its department, and in New York, where city leaders shaved one billion dollars off its six billion dollar police force cost.[13] By cutting these budgets, city and community leaders are beginning to reimagine what policing looks like in the wake of increasing services and programs to prevent violence from happening. While Hollas also advocates for gun reform laws such as owner accountability and smart gun technology to grant access to shooting a weapon (much like fingerprint and facial recognition used on iPhones), she believes defunding efforts will better address systemic issues that affect communities of color as well as concerns within the mental health community. These are two areas where houses of worship are also investing more time and resources, and for good reason.[14]

It's a widely believed misconception that mental illness is to blame for mass shootings. It has been implied and even stated as fact despite numerous studies by medical professionals and the FBI which agree this isn't true. Mass shootings by those with mental illness represent less than 1 percent of annual gun-related homicides according to the American Psychiatric Association. Only 3 percent of violent acts nationwide are perpetuated by someone with a mental illness, and these acts generally don't involve a gun.[15] Perhaps these shooters are immediately thought and reported to have a mental health issue because we simply can't imagine someone in their "right mind" committing such an abominable act. Or perhaps this labeling provides an excuse of some sort as the vast majority of these shooters are white men: Black male shooters are more likely to be described as angry and violent, not insane.

Research indicates that if mental illness is believed to be a factor at all in mass shootings, it's usually one of several drivers or stressors pushing a person to commit such an act, not the underlying cause for it. These drivers are categorized in several ways. Biological factors include a psychiatric illness such as depression or schizophrenia. Psychological and social factors include negative self-image, social isolation, and desire for revenge—all the things we commonly learn about a shooter after the fact.[16] A leading forensic psychiatrist internationally known for his work studying mass shooters interviewed five killers who survived their own attack (generally they expect to be killed or commit suicide during the course of the incident). In a scholarly article published in *Behavioral Sciences & the Law*, Paul Mullen reports all five perpetrators had been bullied or isolated during childhood and displayed levels of suspiciousness, paranoia, and resentfulness. These individuals were prone to hold grudges and fantasize about getting revenge.[17] All of these characteristics are consistent with psychological and social drivers.

While it is possible that undiagnosed biological factors played a part, the acts weren't without the motivation of the psychological and social drivers they all reported. Someone suffering from mental illness without the overriding psychological and social drivers is overwhelming more likely to use a gun to commit suicide rather than to shoot others. In research published by the American Psychiatric Association,

> The rate of stranger homicides committed by individuals with schizophrenia or chronic psychosis is very low. On the basis of meta-analysis from 1999, one stranger homicide is perpetuated by someone with a psychotic illness per year in a population of 14.3 million. Assuming a US population of 320 million, approximately twenty-three people a year on average are killed by an individual with a psychotic illness. In contrast, an average 330 people in the United States are struck by lightning per year. A person is about 15 more times more likely to be

struck by lightning in a given year than to be killed
by a stranger with a diagnosis of schizophrenia or
chronic psychosis.[18]

Those who suffer from mental illness and have access to a gun,
then, are much more likely to be a danger to themselves than to
others. However, targeting those with mental illness histories seems
to be a red herring for groups like the NRA since banning mentally ill persons from purchasing firearms really won't affect their
sales. There are several reasons for this. First, the statistics don't support that this is the demographic buying and using firearms in mass
shootings or violent crime. Second, someone attempting to legally
buy a gun would have to voluntarily disclose a history of civil commitment, insanity, or incompetence since it's often not documented
and is private information. In 2008 the National Instant Criminal
Background Check System Improvement Act was enacted to, among
other things, help better track those with reported cases of mental
illness who should be banned from buying a gun. Under this, the
number of mental health submissions increased tenfold from 2007–
2013.[19] If the mentally ill are largely responsible for mass shootings in
our country, the number of incidents would have decreased during
this period as fewer would have been able to purchase a gun. Not
so. Gun violence actually increased during this period. Following
the Sandy Hook shooting, the office of Sen. Marco Rubio (R-FL)
released this statement:

> In the aftermath of the unspeakable tragedy in
> Newtown, Sen. Rubio, like millions of Americans,
> is looking for public policy changes that would pre-
> vent such a horrible event from happening again.
> He remains a strong supporter of the Second
> Amendment right to safely and responsibly bear
> arms. But he has also always been open to measures
> that would keep guns out of the hands of criminals
> and the mentally ill.[20]

A few days later, executive director of the NRA Wayne LaPierre explicitly made the connection between mass shootings and mental illness in a statement delivered in Washington, DC:

> How many more copycats are waiting in the wings for their moment of fame—from a national media machine that rewards them with the wall-to-wall attention and sense of identity that they crave—while provoking others to try to make their mark? A dozen more killers? A hundred? More? How can we possibly even guess how many, given our nation's refusal to create an active national database of the mentally ill? And the fact is, that wouldn't even begin to address the much larger and more lethal criminal class: Killers, robbers, rapists and drug gang members who have spread like cancer in every community in this country.[21]

I'll give them credit for some wisdom: violent criminals shouldn't have guns. But it's a little hard to heap out praise to the NRA when the mentally ill are lumped in with "killers, robbers, rapists, and drug gang members." Following the mass shooting at the Walmart in El Paso, President Donald Trump stated that "mental illness and hatred pulls the trigger, not the gun."[22] That's an extraordinarily misleading statement. In the United States, one in five adults, or 46.6 million people, experience mental illness each year according to the National Alliance on Mental Illness.[23] Almost none of them commit murder, let alone mass murder. As several journalists have pointed out, imagine if the president had instead said, "Veterans and hatred pulls the trigger, not the gun." The public outcry would have been immediate and severe, but the statement would have been much nearer the truth. In June 2018, the FBI US Department of Justice published the second phase of a study that looked at pre-attack behaviors of active shooters in the US from 2000 to 2013. Using only the cases involving background information that was able to be collected by law enforcement, the second phase examined sixty-three active shooter incidents over the thirteen-year period. It found that of the shooters who were eighteen-years-old and older, 24 percent of them had some military experience, including service in the Army, Navy, Air Force, Marines, and Coast Guard.[24] Other studies have noted that while only 14 percent of adult males in our country have served in the military, around a third of mass shooters have been veterans.[25] Instead of the more productive conversation of how we might better serve our veteran's mental health needs, blanket-blaming mental illness becomes an easy scapegoat for people and organizations that want to appear to be taking meaningful action while ignoring research that negatively affects their consumer base.

We can talk at length about mental health, and we should, but not in arguing whether it causes gun violence, as some would like us to believe. Rather, we need to be talking about mental illness in the context of what we as a community can do to break down the stigma around it and change the culture of how we respond to those suffering with it. According to the National Library of Medicine from the National Institutes of Health, an estimated "6 to 10 percent of all police contacts with the public in the US involve persons with serious mental illnesses" and its findings are "equivocal" that mental illness increases someone's likelihood of being arrested.[26] In another report, this one by the Treatment Advocacy Center, it found someone who suffers from mental illness is sixteen times more likely to be killed in a police encounter.[27] Finding better ways of responding to those with mental illness or in a mental health crisis is one of the factors leading the way in police defunding efforts. Given that our police are often tasked with responding to mental health and wellness-check calls and transporting patients to mental health facilities, all of which are time consuming and sometimes lead to the arrest and incarceration of the person who is then returned to the same community no better or perhaps worse off then before, I can't imagine anyone not being for some kind of reform, police officers included. Cities are now studying models like the one in Eugene, Oregon, where a program called Crisis Assistance Helping Out on the Streets (CAHOOTS) has been operating since 1989. Responders include a medic and a crisis worker, neither of whom carry a gun. Of the 24,000 calls it responded to in 2019, teams were forced to call for police backup in less than 1 percent of cases.[28] Denver launched a similar program called Support Team Assisted Response (STAR) in June 2020, the same month San Francisco's mayor announced non-criminal activity calls would no longer be responded to by the police but rather diverted to other agencies.[29] As cities and communities wrestle with how to better help those in need, places of faith will be called to rethink their own responses now more than ever. The landscape is changing, and churches, mosques, and synagogues—*especially* churches, mosques, and synagogues—should be on the leading edge of how this happens.

Martin Luther King Jr. warned us against sleeping through a revolution, and that the time is always right to do what is right. This message is emphasized in 2 Corinthians 6:2, with God telling the faithful, "'At an acceptable time I have listened to you, and on a day of salvation I have helped you.' See, now is the acceptable time; see, now is the day of salvation!" In both of his uses of the word "time," the apostle Paul uses the Greek word καιρός (kairos), a word that is not about measured chronological time, but about the precise right moment for something to happen. Kelly Brown Douglas leans into the importance of action in this moment: "Kairos time is the right or opportune time. It's a decisive moment in history that potentially has far-reaching impact. It is often a chaotic period, a time of crisis. However, it is through the chaos and crisis that God is fully present, disrupting things as they are and providing an opening for a new future—to God's future."[30] Deanna Hollas agrees that it is in the presence of these tensions that change becomes possible. "That's where I can actually be hopeful for this time, because if we get uncomfortable enough, we'll do something different," she says, noting that in a perfect world her job will no longer be needed.[31] While our planning and preparation are done in hopes of providing safety, our work for justice, equity, and change must be done to lean in further to God's call to us.

Moving Forward

Mental health awareness, gun law reform, and systemic racism weave in and out of these pages more than I expected when I began writing. My question of "How did we get here?" was an important starting point, but "How do we un-get here?" is what we must continue to ask and work to answer.

As Ghandi prompts us, how we can be the change we want to see in the world? In John's first epistle we are enjoined to this because of Christian love: "Little children, let us love, not in word or speech, but in truth and action."[1] How can we do this individually and collectively? Thankfully we have many saints from whom to learn. I think about the "accidental activists" like the students of Stoneman Douglas High School, who find the courage to speak publicly about gun reform, or Susan Bro, the mother of Heather Heyer who was killed by a white supremacist driver at the rally in Charlottesville, who told a Senate panel on May 15, 2019, "This is actually what I mainly do in life, is go around talking to people and saying, 'You have to step up and you have to step out.'"[2] I look at Sharon Risher, who proclaims that Christians cannot sit silently by on issues like mass shootings in our country: "You cannot have social justice without the gospel, and you cannot have the gospel without social justice."[3] I look at programs going on all around our country, big and small, national and local, all intended to move us toward a more just and peaceful world. Life After Hate continues its work to denounce and end white supremacy. Bishops United Against Gun Violence creates powerful liturgies advocates for common sense gun safety measures and holds vigils for the lives lost due to all types of gun violence. Grace Cathedral in San Francisco and other places of worship participate in gun buy-back programs so firearms—some of which are returned to a family after a loved one's suicide—don't go back into circulation. I look to religious centers like the Washington National Cathedral and the Center for the Study of Religion and Conflict (CSRC) at Arizona State University organizing symposia and presenting discussions that help shape conversations in the community, the church, and the world.

As you approach and assess your security and safety planning, I hope you will look to yourself and your congregation and ask what you can do to address the bigger problems. What is your congregation doing to end gun violence? How will your pastoral team help destigmatize those who suffer from mental illness and work toward racial reconciliation in your community? How will you lead others to love and heal and help repair the world? Perhaps the best place to end is with a benediction from Martin Luther King Jr., who reminds us that God is with us in this faithful work:

> Above all, we must be reminded anew that God is at work in his universe. He is not outside the world looking on with a sort of cold indifference. Here on all the roads of life, he is striving in our striving. Like an ever-loving Father, he is working through history for the salvation of his children. As we struggle to defeat the forces of evil, the God of the universe struggles with us. Evil dies on the seashore, not merely because of man's endless struggle against it, but because of God's power to defeat it.[4]

May we give ourselves in faith, prayer, and action as we move toward God's vision of a more loving and peaceful world.

ACKNOWLEDGMENTS

Security and safety are issues I've always been drawn to in my work. I dedicated my ten years as a news reporter to covering "cops, crimes, and courts." It was a beat that kept me busy and all too aware of the dangers and violence in my own community. Despite my days of reporting on tragic incidents and months of sitting through horrific trials, nothing could have prepared me for the emotions I felt following the Sandy Hook school shooting: angry, helpless, and scared. As I wrote in this book, I felt called from that day forward to do whatever I could to help ensure security in the places we expect it most.

There are many, many people to thank for the creation of this book—too many to mention here, but for every long interview or short conversation in passing, thank you. You shaped this book in ways you probably don't even know. However, I would be remiss not to acknowledge the following by name. I must thank St. David's Episcopal Church and the Rev. Chuck Treadwell for letting me do this work. Without his trust and support to address church security, this book wouldn't exist. I give thanks to my husband, Greg, who believes, loves, and supports me in ways I never knew possible, especially while writing a book . . . in quarantine. Above all, I offer unending gratitude for my daughters, Lily and Sophie, who taught me how to love unconditionally and protect fiercely.

Royalties from this book will be donated to Bishops United Against Gun Violence.

Introduction

1 Yolanda Pierce, "Targeting the Sacred: When Houses of Worship Come under Attack" (panel discussion, Center for the Study of Religion and Conflict at Arizona State University, Tempe, Arizona, October 21, 2019).

2 Arno Michaelis quoted in Sharon Risher, *For Such a Time as This: Hope and Forgiveness after the Charleston Massacre* (St. Louis, MO: Chalice Press, 2019), 69.

3 Vera Bergengruen and W. J. Hennigan, "'We Are Being Eaten from Within.' Why America Is Losing the Battle against White Nationalist Terrorism," *Time*, August 8, 2019, https://time .com/5647304/white-nationalist-terrorism-united-states/.

4 Brette Steele, personal interview, April 2, 2020.

5 Zolan Kanno-Youngs, "Homeland Security Dept. Affirms Threat of White Supremacy after Years of Prodding," *New York Times,* October 1, 2019, https://www.nytimes.com/2019/10/01/us /politics/white-supremacy-homeland-security.html.

6 *Confronting Violent White Supremacy (Part 2): Adequacy of the Federal Response, Hearing before the Subcommittee on Civil Rights and Civil Liberties of the Committee on Oversight and Reform*, 116th Cong. (2019) (statement of Rep. Jamie Raskin, chairman of the subcommittee), https://docs.house.gov /meetings/GO/GO02/20190604/109579/HHRG-116-GO02 -Transcript-20190604.pdf.

7 *Confronting Violent White Supremacy (Part 3): Addressing the Transnational Terrorist Threat, Hearing before the Subcommittee on Civil Rights and Civil Liberties of the Committee on Oversight and Reform*, 116th Cong. (2019) (statement of Rep. Stephen Lynch, chairman of the subcommittee on national security), https://www.govinfo.gov/content/pkg/CHRG-116hhrg37975 /html/CHRG-116hhrg37975.htm.

8 Janet Reitman, "US Law Enforcement Failed to See the Threat of White Nationalism. Now They Don't Know How to Stop It," *New York Times Magazine*, November 3, 2018, https://www .nytimes.com/2018/11/03/magazine/FBI-charlottesville-white -nationalism-far-right.html.

9 Ibid.

10 *Confronting White Supremacy (Part I): The Consequences of Inaction, Hearing before the Subcommittee on Civil Rights and Civil Liberties of the Committee on Oversight and Reform*, 116th Cong. (2019) (statement of Omar Ricci, chairman of the Islamic Center of Southern California), https://oversight.house.gov /legislation/hearings/confronting-white-supremacy-part-i-the -consequences-of-inaction.

Chapter 1: What Are We Afraid Of?

1 Joseph Moore, personal interview, March 31, 2020.

2 Scott Bader-Saye, *Formed by Love*, vol. 5, Church's Teaching for a Changing World (New York: Church Publishing, 2017), 90.

3 Ellen Debenport, "Why Do Angels Always Say 'Fear Not?'" New Visions, Patheos.com, December 6, 2016, https://www.patheos .com/blogs/debenport/why-do-the-angels-always-say-fear-not/.

4 Scott Bader-Saye, *Following Jesus in a Culture of Fear: Choosing Trust over Safety in an Anxious Age*, rev. and updated ed. (Grand Rapids, MI: Brazos Press, 2020), 29.

5 Federal Bureau of Investigation Office of Partner Engagement, "Quick Look: 277 Active Shooter Incidents in the United States From 2000 to 2018," FBI.gov, June 9, 2016, https://www.fbi.gov

/about/partnerships/office-of-partner-engagement/active-shooter-incidents-graphics. See also Office of Partner Engagement, "Active Shooter Incidents in the United States in 2019," FBI.gov, April 8, 2020, https://www.fbi.gov/file-repository/active-shooter -incidents-in-the-us-2019-042820.pdf/view.

6 Matt Zapotosky, "Charleston Church Shooter: 'I Would Like to Make It Crystal Clear, I Do Not Regret What I Did,'" *Washington Post*, January 4, 2017, https://www.washingtonpost.com/world /national-security/charleston-church-shooter-i-would-like-to-make -it-crystal-clear-i-do-not-regret-what-i-did/2017/01/04/05b0061e -d1da-11e6-a783-cd3fa950f2fd_story.html.

7 Natalie Barden, personal email, August 29, 2019.

8 Steve Neumann, "I've Developed a Paralyzing, Irrational Fear of Mass Shootings. I Bet I'm Not Alone," First Person, Vox.com, October 2, 2015, https://www.vox.com/2015/9/17/9340679 /mass-shooting-fear.

9 John 14:27b.

10 Bader-Saye, *Following Jesus*, 66.

11 Dietrich Bonhoeffer, "Overcoming Fear," in *The Collected Sermons of Dietrich Bonhoeffer*, ed. Isabelle Best, trans. Claudia D. Bergmann, et al. (Minneapolis, MN: Fortress Press, 2017), cited in Political Theology Network, August 16, 2012, https://politicaltheology.com/overcoming-fear-sermon-dietrich -bonhoeffer/.

12 Robert Schenk, "What to Do with Our Fears," The Dietrich Bonhoeffer Institute, September 19, 2017, https://tdbi.org /devotionals/what-to-do-with-our-fears/.

13 Hannah Devlin, "Unconscious Bias: What Is It and Can It Be Eliminated?" *The Guardian*, December 2, 2018, https://www.theguardian.com/uk-news/2018/dec/02 /unconscious-bias-what-is-it-and-can-it-be-eliminated.

14 Ellen Huet, "Rise of the Bias Busters: How Unconscious Bias Became Silicon Valley's Newest Target," *Forbes*, November 2, 2015, https://www.forbes.com/sites/ellenhuet/2015/11/02

/rise-of- the-bias-busters-how-unconscious-bias-became-silicon
-valleys-newest-target/?sh=399d9aa619b5.

15 Devlin, "Unconscious Bias."

16 Kwame Anthony Appiah, *The Lies That Bind: Rethinking Identity* (New York: Liveright, 2018), 9, 11.

17 Rowan Williams, *Writing in the Dust After September 11* (Grand Rapids, MI: Eerdmans, 2002), 51–52.

18 Umani, personal interview, January 22, 2020.

19 Ibid.

20 Mayo Clinic Staff, "Denial: When It Helps, When It Hurts," Mayo Foundation for Medical Education and Research, April 9, 2020, https://www.mayoclinic.org/healthy-lifestyle/adult-health /in-depth/denial/art-20047926.

21 Psalm 22:14–16.

22 Umani, personal interview.

23 Mintie Betts, "Never Forgotten: Survivors Reflect on Daingerfield Church Shooting Forty Years Later," KETK.com, November 20, 2019, https://www.easttexasmatters.com/news / top-stories/never-forgotten-survivors-reflect-on-daingerfield-church-shooting-40-years-later/.

24 David Schwartz, "Arizona Man Gets Nine Life Terms for Buddhist Temple Murders," Reuters.com, March 14, 2014, https://www.reuters.com/article/us-usa-temple-murder /arizona-man-gets-nine-life-terms-for-buddhist-temple-murders -idUSBREA2D0SB20140314.

25 Aaron Earls, "How Common Are US Church Shootings?" Facts and Trends (Lifeway Research), May 21, 2018, https://factsandtrends.net/2018/05/21/how-likely-are-us -church-shootings/.

26 Gavin de Becker, *The Gift of Fear* (Boston: Little, Brown, 1997), 27–28.

27 Ibid., 28.

28 Martin Luther King Jr., *The Strength to Love* (Philadelphia: Fortress Press, 1981), 117.

Chapter 2: Guns in Sacred Spaces

1 David Hoekema, "A Practical Christian Pacifism," *Christian Century*, October 22, 1986, 917–19, https://www.religion-online .org/article/a-practical-christian-pacifism/.

2 Timothy Tutt, personal interview, January 22, 2020.

3 Aaron Earls, "Half of US Churches Now Enlist Armed Security," *Christianity Today*, January 28, 2020, https://www .christianitytoday.com/news/2020/january/half-of-us-churches -now-enlist-armed-security.html.

4 Tutt, personal interview.

5 Walter Wink, "Nonviolence for the Violent" (transcript of lecture from Spiritual Pilgrimages of Peacemaking retreat in Princeton, New Jersey, February 8, 2008), Lutheran Peace Fellowship, September 10, 2018, https://www.lutheranpeace.org/articles /transcript-of-walter-winks-nonviolence-for-the-violent/.

6 Matthew 5:9–10, 12.

7 Tutt, personal interview.

8 Chuck Treadwell, personal interview, March 2, 2020.

9 Matthew 25:40.

10 Treadwell, personal interview.

11 Ibid.

12 "Amid Rising Attacks on Places of Worship, How Religious Leaders are Responding," PBS News Hour, April 30, 2019, https://www.pbs.org/newshour/show/amid-rising-attacks-on -places-of-worship-how-religious-leaders-are-responding.

13 George Mason, personal email, January 3, 2020.

14 Jim Shepherd, personal interview, March 17, 2020.

15 Matthew 6:19–21.

16 Jake Bleiberg, Jamie Stengle, and NBC 5 Staff, "White Settlement Gunman Grew Angry over Refused Requests for Money: Minister," NBC-DFW, December 31, 2019, https://www.nbcdfw .com/news/local/white-settlement-gunman-grew-angry-over -refused-requests-for-money-minister/2284425/.

17 West Freeway Church of Christ, "Video Shows Security Team Stop Gunman in Texas Church Shooting," *Miami Herald* video, December 30, 2019, https://www.miamiherald.com/ latest-news /article238823983.html.

18 Robert T. Garrett, "Governor Greg Abbott Awards Medal to Armed Deacon Who Stopped White Settlement Church Attack," *Dallas Morning News*, January 13, 2020, https://www .dallasnews.com/news/politics/2020/01/13/gov-greg-abbott -awards-medal-to-armed-deacon-who-stopped-white-settlement -church-attack/.

19 Bleiberg, et al., "White Settlement Gunman."

20 1 Peter 5:8–9, NASB.

21 "Amid Rising Attacks," PBS News Hour.

22 John Blake, "There's Scripture Backing up Trump's Idea to Arm Houses of Worship," CNN, October 29, 2018, https://www.cnn .com/2018/10/28/us/arming-houses-of-worship/index.html.

23 John 10:11–15.

24 Reis Thebault, "Too Small to Hire Guards, Too Worried to Go Gun-Free, Community Churches Are Now Arming Themselves," *Washington Post*, February 14, 2020, https://www.washingtonpost .com/national/too-small-to-hire-guards-too-worried-to-go-gun -free-churches-are-now-arming-themselves/2020/02/14/8eabb574 -3ee9-11ea-baca-eb7ace0a3455_story.html.

25 Joseph Moore, personal interview, March 31, 2020.

26 Ecclesiastes 3:1–8, KJV.

Chapter 3: Faith, Courage, and Mass Tragedy

1 Kevin Sack, "Anguished by 'Spiral of Hate,' Charleston Pastor and Pittsburgh Rabbi Grieve as One," *New York Times*, November 3, 2018, https://www.nytimes.com/2018/11/03/us /pittsburgh-synagogue-charleston-emanuel.html.

2 DeNeen L. Brown and Abby Phillip, "After Tragic Shooting, Charleston Church Reopens with Prayer, Songs and Tears,"

Washington Post, June 21, 2015, https://www.washingtonpost
.com/news/post-nation/wp/2015/06/21/after-tragic-shooting
-charleston-church-reopens-with-prayer-songs-and-tears/.

3 Ibid.

4 Sharon Risher, *For Such a Time as This: Hope and Forgiveness
after the Charleston Massacre* (St. Louis, MO: Chalice Press,
2019), 3.

5 The White House Office of the Press Secretary, "Remarks by
the President in Eulogy for the Honorable Reverend Clementa
Pinckney," June 26, 2015, https://obamawhitehouse.archives.gov
/the-press-office/2015/06/26/remarks-president-eulogy
-honorable-reverend-clementa-pinckney.

6 Rowan Williams, *Writing in the Dust: After September 11*
(Grand Rapids, MI: Eerdmans, 2002), 7–8.

7 Kelly Brown Douglas, *Stand Your Ground: Black Bodies and the
Justice of God* (Maryknoll, NY: Orbis Books, 2015), 168.

8 Elie Wiesel, *Night*, trans. Marion Wiesel (New York: Hill and
Wang, 2006), 76.

9 Ibid., 66.

10 Ibid., 91.

11 Jenni Frazer, "Wiesel: Yes, We Really Did Put God on Trial,"
Jewish Chronicle, September 19, 2008, https://www.thejc.com
/news/uk/wiesel-yes-we-really-did-put-god-on-trial-1.5056.

12 Scott Bader-Saye, personal interview, June 12, 2019.

13 Gavin de Becker, *Gift of Fear* (Boston: Little, Brown, 1997), 28.

14 Martin Luther King Jr., *Strength to Love* (Philadelphia: Fortress
Press, 1981), 119.

15 White House Office of the Press Secretary, "Remarks by the
President."

16 Ibid.

17 Madison Park, "A Year after Mass Shooting, Charleston Church
Embraces Its Community," CNN, June 17, 2016, https://www
.cnn.com/2016/06/17/us/charleston-mass-shooting-anniversary
/index.html.

18 Campbell Robertson, "Pittsburgh Marks a Massacre's Anniversary with Prayers and Projects," *New York Times*, October 27, 2019, https://www.nytimes.com/2019/10/27/us/tree -of-life-shooting-anniversary.html.

19 Tim Ciesco, "'God Wastes Nothing': Wedgwood Baptist Church Commemorates Twenty-Year Anniversary of Deadly Shooting," NBC-DFW, September 15, 2019, https://www.nbcdfw.com /news/local/god-wastes-nothing-wedgwood-baptist-church -commemorates-20-year-anniversary-of-deadly-shootings/1964246/.

20 Risher, *For Such a Time as This*, 47.

21 Ibid., 56.

22 Bernhard W. Anderson and Steven Bishop, *Out of the Depths: The Psalms Speak for Us Today*, 3rd ed. (Louisville, KY: Westminster John Knox, 2000), 60.

Chapter 4: Our Duty to Protect

1 Chuck Treadwell, personal interview, March 2, 2020.

2 Walter Wink, *Jesus and Nonviolence: A Third Way* (Minneapolis: Fortress Press, 2003), 15–16.

3 Ibid., 27–29.

4 Kelly Brown Douglas, *Stand Your Ground: Black Bodies and the Justice of God* (Maryknoll, NY: Orbis Books, 2015), 184–85.

5 Martin Luther King Jr., "My Pilgrimage to Nonviolence," Martin Luther King, Jr. Research and Education Institute, Stanford University, first published in *Fellowship* 24 (September 1, 1958): 4–9, https://kinginstitute.stanford.edu/king-papers/documents /my-pilgrimage-nonviolence.

6 Wink, *Jesus and Nonviolence*, 78–79.

7 Christian Picciolini, "My Descent into America's Neo-Nazi Movement—and How I Got Out," filmed in November 2017 in Denver, Colorado, TED video, 20:10, https://www.ted.com /talks/christian_picciolini_my_descent_into_america_s_neo _nazi_movement_and_how_i_got_out.

8 Ibid.

9 Arno Michaelis, The Forgiveness Project, https://www
.theforgivenessproject.com/stories/arno-michaels/.

10 Picciolini, "My Descent."

11 Glenn Smith, Jennifer Berry Hawes, and Abigail Darlington,
"Testimony Shows Dylann Roof Scouted Emanuel AME Church
for Months before Mass Shooting," *The Post and Courier*,
December 13, 2016, https://www.postandcourier.com
/church_shooting/testimony-shows-dylann-roof-scouted-emanuel
-ame-church-for-months-before-mass-shooting/article_ ce5fa596
-c12d-11e6-903b-974d94ad04f3.html.

12 Ian Douglas, personal interview, February 26, 2020.

13 Neil Blumofe, personal interview, August 22, 2020.

14 Psalm 137:1–4.

15 Blumofe, personal interview.

16 John 10:27.

17 Ema Rosero-Nordalm, "Dr. Catherine Meeks," National
Episcopal Church Women, April 16, 2020, https://ecwnational
.org/an-interview-with-dr-catherine-meeks/.

Chapter 5: Our Call to Welcome

1 Stephane Fitch, "How to Reduce Bank Robberies," *Forbes*,
November 12, 2009, https://www.forbes.com/forbes/2009/1130
/outfront-bank-robbery-crime-how-to-reduce-robberies
.html#2049e4fd7f17.

2 Tom Field, "SafeCatch: How to Deter Bank Robberies—
Interview with FBI Special Agent Larry Carr," BankInfoSecurity
.com, August 25, 2009, https://www.bankinfosecurity.com
/interviews/safecatch-how-to-deter-bank-robberies-interview
-fbi-special-agent-i-324.

3 Ibid.

4 Ibid.

5 James Densley and Simon Osamoh, "How to Stop Violence in Places of Worship," MinnPost.com, November 13, 2017, https://www.minnpost.com/community-voices/2017/11/how -stop-violence-places-worship/.

6 Neil Blumoffe, personal interview, August 20, 2020.

7 Densley and Osamoh, "How to Stop Violence."

8 Chris Story and Chuck Randolph, "Protecting Houses of Worship with Bryan Flannery," January 9, 2020, *Conversations in Close Protection*, podcast audio, https://podcasts.apple.com /us/podcast/bonus-episode-protecting-houses-worship-bryan -flannery/.id1464565197?i=1000462073050.

9 Ibid.

10 Hebrews 13:2.

11 Stephen S. Pearce, "Judge a Society by Its Hospitality," ReformJudaism.org, https://reformjudaism.org/learning/torah -study/torah-commentary/judge-society-its-hospitality.

12 Benedict, "Chapter 53: The Reception of Guests," The Holy Rule of St. Benedict (Benedictine Abbey of Christ in the Desert), accessed March 20, 2021, https://christdesert.org/prayer/rule-of -st-benedict/chapter-53-the-reception-of-guests/.

13 Tim Tutt, personal interview, January 22, 2020.

14 Scott Bader-Saye, personal interview, June 12, 2019.

15 Blumhofe, personal interview.

16 Chuck Treadwell, personal interview, March 2, 2020.

17 JoAnn A. Post, "Church Security and the Risks of Hospitality," *Christian Century*, May 1, 2019, https://www.christiancentury. org/article/first-person/church-security-and-risks-of-hospitality.

Chapter 6: Making a Plan

1 Genesis 41:38–40.

2 Matthew 25:1–4.

3 Matthew 25:1–3.

4 Aaron Earls, "Half of US Churches Now Enlist Armed Security," *Christianity Today*, January 28, 2020, https://www .christianitytoday.com/news/2020/january/half-of-us-churches -now-enlist-armed-security.html.

5 Acts 6:3–4, NIV.

6 Martin Luther King Jr., *Strength to Love* (Philadelphia: Fortress Press, 1981, 13.

7 Ibid., 18.

8 Rob Sokol, personal interview, March 2, 2020.

9 Ryan Lindsay, "His Aunt Saw Red Flags, Police Got a Risk Warrant," *Connecticut Mirror*, October 7, 2019, https://ctmirror .org/2019/10/07/his-aunt-saw-red-flags-police-got-a-risk-warrant/.

10 Mark Berman, "After Pittsburgh Synagogue Attack, Jewish Groups, Security Officials Prepare to Confront Future Violence," *Washington Post*, April 9, 2019, https://www.washingtonpost .com/national/after-pittsburgh-synagogue-attack-jewish-groups -security-officials-prepare-to-confront-future-violence/2019/04/09 /bf9f9c62-5af7-11e9-842d-7d3ed7eb3957_story.html.

11 Amy Sowder, "Episcopalians Balance Fear with Preparation in the Wake of US Mass Shootings," Episcopal News Service, April 19, 2018, https://www.episcopalnewsservice.org/2018/04/19 /episcopalians-balance-fear-with-preparation-in-the-wake-of-u-s -mass-shootings/.

Chapter 7: Common Planning Pitfalls

1 Kaitlin Roig-DeBellis, *Choosing Hope* (New York: G.P. Putnam's Sons, 2015), 146–47.

2 Isaiah 43:1–2.

3 Isaiah 43:18–19.

4 Leslie Marmon Silko, *Ceremony* (New York: Penguin, 1986), 126.

5 Martin Luther King Jr., *Strength to Love* (Philadelphia: Fortress Press, 1981, 15.

6 Matthew 10:9–10.

7 David Brown, interview with church and mosque leaders in Texas, January 4, 2019, *Texas Standard* podcast audio, https://www.texasstandard.org/stories/texas-standard-for-january-4-2019/.

8 G. Jeffrey MacDonald, "How Should Churches Protect Their People?" *Living Church*, March 29, 2019, https://livingchurch.org/2019/03/29/how-should-churches-protect-their-people/.

9 Rob Sokol, personal interview, March 2, 2020.

Chapter 8: Social Justice and Cultural Change

1 CNN, "Raw Video: Obama on Senate Rejecting Gun Measure," YouTube video, 14:18, April 17, 2013, https://www.youtube.com/watch?v=MQGoyQ-TXwo&feature=emb_logo.

2 Ian Douglas, personal interview, February 26, 2020.

3 Ian T. Douglas, "Religious Questions from Sandy Hook: How Do We Make Sense of This?" Huffpost.com, December 18, 2012, https://www.huffpost.com/entry/religious-questions-from-sandy-hook-how-do-we-make-sense-of-this_b_2324161.

4 Tzvi Freeman, "What Is Tikkun Olam?" Chabad.org, https://www.chabad.org/library/article_cdo/aid/3700275/jewish/What-Is-Tikkun-Olam.htm.

5 Tom Richell, "'Welcome to the Revolution': Watch Cameron Kasky's Passionate March for Our Lives Speech in Full," *Independent*, March 24, 2018, https://www.independent.co.uk/news/world/americas/march-our-lives-washington-cameron-kasky-video-parkland-florida-school-shooting-marjory-stoneman-douglas-a8272231.html.

6 Martin Luther King Jr., "Remaining Awake through a Great Revolution" (speech, Washington National Cathedral, March 31, 1968), accessed March 20, 2021, https://kinginstitute.stanford.edu/king-papers/publications/knock-midnight-inspiration-great-sermons-reverend-martin-luther-king-jr-10.

7 Vann Newkirk, "A Long, Long Way: Race and Film—*Get Out*" (panel discussion, Washington National Cathedral, February 17, 2018).

8 Kelly Brown Douglas, *Stand Your Ground: Black Bodies and the Justice of God* (Maryknoll, NY: Orbis Books, 2015), 223.

9 Ibid., 225.

10 Phillip A. Jackson, "Choosing Jesus or Barabbas: Reflecting on Gun Violence in America" (sermon, Trinity Episcopal Church, Wall Street, March 28, 2018), https://fb.watch/5yvnnqNFI8/.

11 Ibid.

12 Deanna Hollas, personal interview, October 16, 2020.

13 Meena Venkataramanan, "Austin City Council Cuts Police Department Budget by One-Third, Mainly through Reorganizing Some Duties out from Law Enforcement Oversight," *The Texas Tribune*, August 13, 2020, https://www.texastribune. org/2020/08/13/austin-city-council-cut-police-budget-defund/.

14 Hollas, personal interview.

15 James L. Knoll IV and George D. Annas, *Gun Violence and Mental Illness* (American Psychiatric Association Publishing, 2016), 81, https://psychiatryonline.org/doi/pdf/10.5555/appi .books.9781615371099.

16 Ibid., 86.

17 Paul E. Mullen, "The Autogenic (Self-Generated) Massacre," *Behavioral Sciences & the Law* 22, no. 3 (2004–5): 311–23.

18 Knoll and Annas, *Gun Violence*, 90–91.

19 Dylan Matthews, "Stop Blaming Mental Illness for Mass Shootings," Vox.com, August 5, 2019, https://www.vox.com /policy-and-politics/2017/11/9/16618472/mental-illness-gun -homicide-mass-shootings.

20 Daniel Strauss, "Rubio Supports 'Comprehensive Study' of Gun Laws," *The Hill*, December 17, 2012, https://thehill .com/blogs/blog-briefing-room/news/273273-rubio-supports -comprehensive-study-of-gun-laws.

21 "NRA: Full Statement by Wayne LaPierre in Response to Newtown Shootings." *Guardian*, https://www.theguardian.com /world/2012/dec/21/nra-full-statement-lapierre-newtown.

22 Jacqueline Howard, "Blaming Mass Shootings on Mental Illness is 'Inaccurate' and 'Stigmatizing,' Experts Say," CNN, August 5, 2019, https://www.cnn.com/2019/08/05/health/mass-shootings -mental-illness-trump/index.html.

23 Ibid.

24 Sarah Craun, James Silver, and Andre Simons, "A Study of the Pre-Attack Behaviors of Active Shooters in the United States Between 2000 and 2013," Federal Bureau of Investigation, US Department of Justice, Washington, DC, 2018, 7, https://www .fbi.gov/file-repository/pre-attack-behaviors-of-active-shooters -in-us-2000-2013.pdf.

25 Elizabeth Howe, "There's a Statistical Link between Military Experience and Mass Shooters," ConnectingVetsRadio.com, November 9, 2018, https://connectingvets.radio.com/articles /link-between-military-experience-and-mass-shootings.

26 Matthew Roza, "Why Defunding the Police Means Investing in Mental Health," Salon.com, August 11, 2020, https://www.salon .com/2020/08/11/why-defunding-the-police-means-investing-in -mental-health/.

27 Meera Jagannathan, "As Activists Call to Defund the Police, Mental Health Advocates Say 'The Time is Now' to Rethink Public Safety," MarketWatch.com, June 19, 2020, https://www .marketwatch.com/story/long-before-defund-the-police-mental -health-advocates-have-been-redefining-public-safety-2020-06-11.

28 Grace Hauck, "Police Have Shot People Experiencing a Mental Health Crisis. Who Should You Call Instead?" *USA Today*, September 8, 2020, https://www.usatoday.com/story/news /nation/2020/09/18/police-shooting-mental-health-solutions -training-defund/5763145002/.

29 Matt Vasilogambros, "'If the Police Aren't Needed, Let's Leave Them Out Completely,'" *Stateline*, PewTrusts.org, June 23, 2020, https://www.pewtrusts.org/en/research-and-analysis/blogs /stateline/2020/06/23/if-the-police-arent-needed-lets-leave-them -out-completely.

30 Brown Douglas, *Stand Your Ground*, 219.

31 Hollas, personal interview.

Conclusion: Moving Forward

1 1 John 3:18.

2 *Confronting White Supremacy (Part I): The Consequences of Inaction, Hearing before the Subcommittee on Civil Rights and Civil Liberties of the Committee on Oversight and Reform*, 116th Cong. (2019) (statement of Susan Bro, cofounder, president, and board chair), https://docs.house.gov/meetings/go/go02/20190515 /109478/hhrg-116-go02-wstate-bros-20190515-u2.pdf.

3 Sharon Risher, *For Such a Time as This: Hope and Forgiveness after the Charleston Massacre* (St. Louis, MO: Chalice Press, 2019), 98–99.

4 Martin Luther King Jr., *Strength to Love* (Philadelphia: Fortress Press, 1981, c. 1963), 84.

CPSIA information can be obtained
at www.ICGtesting.com
Printed in the USA
JSHW052132300721
17380JS00005B/6

9 781640 653221